Please read this important book. This book provides a "red flag warning" to Southern Baptists regarding the disastrous outcome of the Great Commission Resurgence. Steep decline and diminished cooperation are the fruit of the GCR. The essential questions are: "Will Southern Baptists admit the mistakes made as a result of GCR; and will they address those mistakes and chart new paths?"

Randy Adams
Executive Director, Northwest Baptist Convention

Chuck Kelley has been a life-long Southern Baptist who served for many years as President of New Orleans Baptist Seminary. With a heartbeat for Evangelism and a deep concern for Southern Baptists today and in the future, he has penned a must-read book. The provocative title says it all: *The Best Intentions: How a Plan to Revitalize the SBC Accelerated Its Decline.* Relying on official SBC data reports year by year since 2010, Kelley points to an SBC in serious decline that is accelerating in virtually all areas of Baptist life. With a major focus on the North American Mission Board and church planting, he demonstrates that the "Great Commission Resurgence" Plan over the past decade has not been working. Lessons learned and possible future directions conclude the book. It is no secret that the Southern Baptist Convention is struggling. This book explains some of the reasons why. Every Southern Baptist should read this book.

David L. Allen, PhD
Distinguished Professor of Practical Theology
Dean, Adrian Rogers Center for Biblical Preaching
Mid-America Baptist Theological Seminary, Memphis, TN

Southern Baptists are known as a family of autonomous churches that come together with the only purpose of advancing the Great Commission. The way we accomplish this is by sending missionaries at home and abroad through a mystical yet practical system that connects us all: the Cooperative Program. Sadly, in recent years we have seen a decline not only in membership and giving, but also the deterioration of our institutional consistency. In this well-researched book Dr. Kelley challenges us to reexamine with all honesty the results of the Great Commission Resurgence while pointing out the urgent need for a great conservative revival.

Javier Chavez, PhD
Senior Pastor, Amistad Cristiana International Gainesville, GA

With strength from his depth of years in careful research and a keen understanding of Southern Baptist life, Charles Kelley, a seasoned Southern Baptist leader, has provided perhaps the most astute assessment of the work of the Southern Baptist Convention in recent history. Millions of Christians call the SBC their spiritual home. For some time now, many have noticed the darkening storm clouds gathering in the distance. Kelley adeptly demonstrates that the storm is no longer distant, but that it has already begun to thunder and rain with intensifying ferocity. What remains to be seen is whether or not the historic and unprecedented work of Southern Baptists will survive this impending tempest. You don't want to miss his startling assessment. Read it with eyes open.

Z. Scott Colter, PhD
Assistant Professor, Mid-America Theological Seminary
Executive Director, Conservative Baptist Network
Partner, Colter & Co.

The language of the "Great Commission Resurgence" was noble and well-intended, but "the road to disintegration can be paved with good intentions." And I thank Dr. Kelley for so aptly demonstrating this.

Mark Coppenger, PhD
Pastor, Author, Educator, SBC Leader

Every Southern Baptist needs to carefully read and intensely reflect on the assessment of Dr. Chuck Kelley regarding the current state of affairs in the Southern Baptist Convention. His research is right on point and profoundly insightful. Finally someone is bringing to light what no one has been willing to address until now. The question is, "What will we do about these revealed truths?"

Jerry Drace
Senior Pastor, Friendship Baptist Church, Friendship, TN

Having the best intended, and biblical, goals of winning the lost throughout the world by means of the Great Commission Resurgence of the Southern Baptist Convention a decade ago, apparently are not working. Chuck Kelley has provided a sobering critique of how the Resurgence is progressing.

It examines the aims and goals of the Resurgence against actual data since its formal adoption. The picture he paints is not pleasant. The SBC is in decline despite our Best Intentions. This is a must read for members of the churches, pastors, professors, and seminary students to recognize, that while we are trying to fulfill Christ's great commission, we are failing. Serious discussions in churches, colleges, seminaries should form circles of concern and design changed strategic steps to realign with our desire to seeing all people come to Christ.

Keith E. Eitel, PhD
Retired Professor of Missions and World Christian Studies,
Southwestern Baptist Theological Seminary

In his book, Dr. Chuck Kelley delivers a searing critique of the Southern Baptist Convention's disastrous handling of the Great Commission Resurgence report, which was approved for implementation in 2010. Rather than resurgence, there has been an accelerated regression. The most significant change that has occurred since then is the North American Board's drastic shift away from a cooperative, regional approach to church planting and evangelism, in favor of a narrow strategy that emphasizes central control and minimizes evangelism resourcing. Kelley painstakingly documents the unprecedented decline that has occurred during this decade, making this book a must-read for any Southern Baptist who values transparency, cooperation, and effective use of mission funds.

Dr. Bobby Gilstrap
Founder, Dynamic Church Ministries, Inc.
Former Executive Director of Baptist State Convention of Michigan

In *The Best Intentions: How A Plan to Revitalize the SBC Accelerated Its Decline*, Dr. Chuck Kelley provides a comprehensive analysis of the Great Commission Resurgence initiative proposed and approved at the 2010 SBC Annual Meeting. Dr. Kelley draws on his expertise as a distinguished research professor of evangelism to provide a critical and objective dissection of the GCR motion and its 10-year impact on the SBC. This book accurately details why a motion that started out with good intentions rapidly turned into one of the most destructive initiatives ever approved by SBC Messengers. The sad truth is, as detailed by Dr. Kelley, it continues to negatively impact the SBC. This book is informative, jolting, eye-opening, and a must-read for every Southern Baptist.

James Gregory
Pastor
SBC Executive Committe Officer
UISBC President

In Dr. Charles Kelley's new book, *The Best Intentions: How A Plan to Revitalize the SBC Accelerated Its Decline*, he has thoughtfully and methodically evaluated the results of the Great Commission Task Force recommendations and provided a clear analysis of where Southern Baptists are today compared to 2010 when the Convention adopted the Task Force's report.

While Dr. Kelley contends that faithful Southern Baptists wanted to devise a strategy to rescue the Convention from an obvious decline, the seven recommendations have not reversed the downward trend as one might hope. The writer correctly explains that the root of the problem is that the Task Force envisioned the SBC as an organization that functioned like a church when its actual purpose is to create a cooperative synergy out of the work of autonomous, independent churches and entities - that the focus should be on coordinated effort, not coordinated management.

Dr. Kelley's book clearly points out that two of the major concerns among the recommendations pertains to Great Commission giving and the phasing out of all Cooperative Agreements between NAMB and the state conventions. The book implies that these two issues have compromised the cooperative synergy between the states and the national convention. The author also wisely points out that the new emphasis on church planting presupposes evangelism would happen without giving it much attention. Unfortunately, there is no evidence that a great soul winning effort has emerged out of the church planting emphasis.

J. Gerald Harris
Pastor for 41 years
Former editor of The Christian Index

The urgency of the hour that we live in needs to move us to be ever-more on mission to share the hope of Jesus with our communities, nation, and world. This extremely insightful resource from Dr. Chuck Kelley is valuable on multiple levels for Southern Baptist pastors and churches who are committed to the Great Commission call of Christ.

Dr. Brad Jurkovich
Senior Pastor, First Baptist Church, Bossier City, LA
Spokesman, Conservative Baptist Network

A lawyer friend once said, "Facts are stubborn things." Dr. Kelley, in his book, *The Best Intentions*, has meticulously stuck to the facts. The fact is that the statistics for the Southern Baptist Convention reveal there has been a dramatic decrease in the number of baptisms over the last decade. The heart and soul of Southern Baptists is the salvation of the lost that is evidenced by baptisms. Dr. Kelley asks an important question: Is it time to evaluate the successfulness of the Southern Baptist Convention implementation of the Great Commission Resurgence strategic plan? It is an honest question. In reading this book, you will be challenged to answer that question. It is not a book of "blame" but one of introspection. As a pastor, staff at the North American Mission Board, and member of the Great Commission Taskforce, I welcome an honest review of where we are as Southern Baptists. To ignore the "facts" is to fail. In his book, *Smart Thinking for Crazy Times: The Art of Solving the Right Problems,* Ian I. Mitroff's proposition is that we solve the "wrong problems" precisely. The conclusion is we are good at problem solving but not good at problem identifying. Dr. Kelley has identified a critical problem: evangelism is not a priority for Southern Baptists according to the statistics. It is time to "solve" this problem correctly. The "best intentions" are not sufficient.

Harry Lewis
Kingdom First Ministries

With the knowledge of an investigative reporter on 60 Minutes, Dr. Charles Kelley does his homework on the decline of baptisms and giving in the SBC the past twenty years. His findings are backed up by accurate charts and reports from the floor of our annual Southern Baptist Convention. The findings should concern all Southern Baptists who take seriously the Great Commission given to us by Jesus and what has always been a priority for our convention. We would encourage all Southern Baptists to read this book, be convicted by the declining reports in this book, repent of our "Best Intentions," and ask God to once again send revival through the Southern Baptist Convention.

Fred Luter, Jr.
Senior Pastor, Franklin Avenue Baptist Church, New Orleans, LA
Former President of the Southern Baptist Convention
Chip Luter
Senior Associate Pastor, Franklin Avenue Baptist Church

Dr. Kelley writes with the mind of a scholar, the heart of a statesman, and the soul of an evangelist. I wrote and voted against the GCR recommendations, foreseeing the very consequences outlined in this book. The research here unfortunately proves we have indeed had a Great Commission Regression. This is a sobering but needful read for every Southern Baptist!

Mike Stone
Senior Pastor, Emmanuel Baptist Church, Blackshear, GA

Speaking the truth in love is not always easy, but it is essential. Dr. Kelley's assessment marshals the critical evidence compelling us to ask what has happened to our convention and our strategic evangelistic objectives. This siren call cries for an honest examination, evaluation, and transformation of our strategic cooperative agreements in order to reinvigorate our cooperative efforts to reach the world for Christ. Hopefully, it is not too late, for we all long to hear our Lord's commendation, "Well done, good and faithful!"

Dr. Chris Thompson
Pastor, South River Baptist Church

Those of us who know and respect Dr. Chuck Kelley are not surprised by his latest book. Both irenic and thorough, it gives an eye-opening and hopeful account of the current state of The Southern Baptist Convention. Whether one agrees with his conclusions or not, all will be helped by his excellent analyses.

Jerry Vines
Pastor Emeritus, First Baptist Church, Jacksonville, FL
Two-time President, Southern Baptist Convention

Proverbs 14:12 says, "there is a way that seems right to a person but in the end it leads to death." Many decisions, even well thought out ones, on the surface appear to be wise, prudent, and selfless.

Over time, the results of such decisions prove otherwise. Rather than face the arduous, and quite frankly unpleasant task of admitting and addressing the downward trends, leaders choose to maintain the status quo while seeing the same results.

Chuck Kelley, once again, is calling for an honest and frank discussion about the institutionalization of the SBC caused by a failure to keep the main thing the main thing, which is the SBC does not exist for itself but for those who have yet to come to faith in Jesus.

Dr. Mike Whitson

Pastor of Indian Trail Baptist Church, Indian Trail, NC

The Best
Intentions

The Best Intentions

How a Plan to Revitalize
the SBC Accelerated
Its Decline

Charles S. Kelley Jr

NORTHEASTERN BAPTIST PRESS

Bennington, Vermont

The Best Intentions
How a Plan to Revitalize the SBC Accelerated Its Decline
Copyright © 2023 by Charles S. Kelley, Jr.

Published by Northeastern Baptist Press
Post Office Box 4600
Bennington, VT 05201

Scripture quotations are taken from various translations and indicated at each reference.

Cover design by Leason Stiles

Softcover ISBN: 978-1-953331-27-4
Ebook ISBN: 978-1-953331-28-1

One should be careful not to evaluate major change too quickly. Change always comes with negative perceptions because it tends to unsettle the settled. But, there is one thing worse than evaluating change too quickly. That one thing worse is being so invested in implementing major change that one fails to evaluate honestly its effect.

TABLE OF CONTENTS

FOREWORD
BY ROBERT JEFFRESS ——————————— i

EXECUTIVE SUMMARY ——————— v

ABBREVIATIONS ————————— ix

PART ONE:
THE SET UP ———————————————— 1

Who Are Southern Baptists? ——————— 3

What Do Southern Baptists Do? ————— 7

Prelude to the Great
Commission Resurgence ————————— 14

Birth of the Great Commission Resurgence — 20

PART TWO:
THE GREAT COMMISSION
RESURGENCE PROPOSALS ——————— 27

Component One:
Getting the Mission Right ——————— 29

Component Two:
Making Our Values Transparent ————— 34

Component Three:
Encouraging Cooperative Program Giving
and Other Great Commission Giving ——— 39

Component Four:
Reaching North America ———————— 70

Component Five:
Reaching Unreached and Underserved
People Groups in North America —————— 133

Component Six:
Promoting the Cooperative Program
and Elevating Stewardship —————— 139

Component Seven:
The Calling of the Nations
and the SBC Allocation Budget —————— 152

Miscellaneous Matters —————— 156

PART THREE:
REFLECTIONS —————— 159

Summary —————— 161

Lessons Learned from the
Great Commission Resurgence —————— 166

The Last Word —————— 196

FOREWORD
BY JUNIOR HILL —————— 199

A PERSONAL TESTIMONY
FROM MARK COPPENGER —————— 201

APPENDIX I :
CORRESPONDENCE BETWEEN STATE
CONVENTION EXECUTIVES, THE
NORTH AMERICAN MISSION BOARD,
AND THE SBC EXECUTIVE COMMITTEE ——— 205

APPENDIX II:
SBC DATA CHARTS —————— 215

FOREWORD

By Robert Jeffress

Jesus came "to seek and to save those who were lost" (Luke 19:10). What motivated Jesus must remain the mandate of the church in every era. Dr. Chuck Kelley, having served as president of the New Orleans Baptist Theological Seminary for twenty-three years, has never ceased to be an evangelist during his years as an SBC leader. And I candidly admit that the challenge of following the path of Truett, Criswell, and others who served before me at the First Baptist Church of Dallas has demonstrated to me repeatedly my own inadequacy under the shadow of the greatness of our God. But of all the opportunities and challenges I have faced, the one that ignites my soul is the incredible number of people who continue to be turned to Christ through the local and international ministries of our church. That is how it ought to be! Above all else, the church is about getting the message of salvation to precious people by every means possible and seeing them commit themselves to the Lord God.

Whether we examine attendance records, number of baptisms, or any other marker in our Southern Baptist Convention, one thing is crystal clear–as a denomination, we are now failing our Lord and accomplishing far less than we did only a few years ago. Dr. Kelley, in this short monograph entitled *The Best Intentions*, examines how things that no one intended to happen came to be part of what developed under the aegis of the Great Commission Resurgence, approved by the Convention in 2010.

Kelley invites his beloved Southern Baptist brethren to engage in a serious conversation about the Great Commission of our Lord. He is certain that such an examination will include a careful analysis of the initiatives adopted by the Convention as well as a careful investigation of official reports on the results spanning ten years. The question needs to avoid Southern Baptist politics and focus on Southern Baptist fruitfulness. The question to be honestly considered is whether or not the proposed and implemented strategies are actually working. If these efforts are not working, how can the Convention and its churches recover the strategy of the New Testament in reaching a lost world for Christ?

We Baptists are poised on a cultural divide. As we look to the future, we can create within our Baptist house another division like the United Methodist Church, or we can choose to return to the New Testament and recreate a thirst for the souls of our confused world. Thank you, Dr. Kelley for fearlessly pointing the way to revival!

Robert Jeffress
Pastor, First Baptist Church
Dallas, TX

EXECUTIVE SUMMARY

Southern Baptists, we need to talk! We are accustomed to hearing rosy progress reports from SBC leaders. The time has come to talk about the realities of the tangled mass of thorns and weeds underneath some of today's rosy reports. We need to talk about both the strategies we propose and the outcomes over time that we actually receive. We need to pay attention to those outcomes. Disappointing outcomes are reasons for strategic adjustments, not angry fights. Attempts to address unexpected outcomes are not a search for conflict. The Southern Baptist Convention is not a tool for managing autonomous churches, conventions, and entities. The Convention is a tool for enlisting independent churches in a mighty cooperative effort to seek the salvation of every person on earth through Jesus Christ and to overwhelm the darkness of a broken world with the radiance of disciples living their lives in accordance with God's Word. We do that best when the outcomes of our strategies inspire us.

Southern Baptists are a family of churches that did the unthinkable, trading the glory and immediate satisfaction of acting alone for the immense power unleashed by cooperation, embracing the same mission (the Great Commission) and paying for it with a common purse (the Cooperative Program). This book attempts to set the stage for that much needed conversation about where the SBC is today in its Great Commission progress. This work cannot address every thorn or weed under those rosy reports, but it can provide a place to start talking.

The Southern Baptist Convention is not a tool for managing autonomous churches, conventions, and entities. The Convention is a tool for enlisting independent churches in a mighty cooperative effort to seek the salvation of every person on earth through Jesus Christ and to overwhelm the darkness of a broken world with the radiance of disciples living their lives in accordance with God's Word. We do that best when the outcomes of our strategies inspire us.

In the summer of 2009, a Georgia pastor was elected President of the Southern Baptist convention. With the best intentions, the newly elected SBC president sought to generate fresh interest in the Great Commission by:

- Changing the SBC funding process;
- Redefining the relationship between the North American Mission Board and the state conventions and regional associations; and
- Making a dramatic shift away from direct evangelism and to church planting.

To indicate the desire for transformative change, the name chosen for this effort was the Great Commission Resurgence (GCR), in hope that it would affect the Convention as deeply as did the Conservative resurgence in earlier decades. In spite of having the best intentions, the decade following the adoption of the Great Commission Resurgence proved to be more of a Great Commission Regression. This assessment will:

In spite of having the best intentions, the decade following the adoption of the Great Commission Resurgence proved to be more of a Great Commission Regression.

- Describe each component of the Great Commission Resurgence proposals;
- Identify the outcomes after a decade of implementation, and;

- Provide charts drawn from official SBC data reports to document the unprecedented decline that deepened and accelerated across all areas of SBC life.

Readers will be able to see for themselves that the plan did not work as expected. The report concludes with lessons learned from the assessment and suggestions about where the SBC goes from here. The crucial question:

Is the Convention willing to begin talking about adjustments and changes to its strategic approach to the Great Commission?

Charles S. Kelley Jr.

ABBREVIATIONS

CP:	Cooperative Program
CR:	Conservative Resurgence
EC:	Executive Committee
GCR:	Great Commission Resurgence
HMB:	Home Mission Board
IMB:	International Mission Board
NAMB:	North American Mission Board
SBC:	Southern Baptist Convention
VP:	Vice President
WMU:	Woman's Missionary Union

Part One:

The Set Up

Who Are Southern Baptists?

The Southern Baptist Convention (SBC) is the largest Protestant (non-Catholic) family of churches in the United States. In various ways, the SBC differs significantly from other major American church families. The actual Southern Baptist Convention only exists for two days each year, when messengers (representatives) from the churches choosing to participate gather in some city for an annual meeting to "rally the troops," conduct necessary business, and hear progress reports from SBC entities. The identity of the messengers varies widely from year to year. Every Convention includes messengers who attend nearly every year, messengers attending periodically–often based on the location of the meeting or its agenda–and messengers attending their first ever SBC. Thus, each SBC annual meeting is a different and newly formed body gathered to maintain the historical continuity of a family of churches formed in 1845.

Having messengers in attendance at the annual meeting is not required for Convention membership. When qualified churches request membership in the Convention, they are assigned an SBC ID number. The church retains that number until such a time as either the church or the Convention decides to withdraw membership. Every SBC church, large or small, is completely autonomous with no directive or supervisory authority beyond the local congregation. These autonomous churches voluntarily cooperate together to operate twelve autonomous entities, each with its own independent set of Trustees, to provide theological education to thousands of students and to engage in the missionary enterprise on a very large scale in the United States and abroad.

The SBC elects all entity Trustees and assigns particular parameters for ministry (i.e., their ministry statement) to each entity. Other than that, the respective Trustee bodies are alone responsible for all ministry operations of each entity. There is no external directive or supervisory authority beyond its own Board of Trustees. The twelve entities are funded in part from a common purse created by voluntary gifts from the member churches of the SBC. That common purse is called the Cooperative Program (CP). In addition, CP funds the Baptist state conventions and their ministries (also autonomous) formed by SBC churches in a region. Local SBC churches in all fifty states participate in the Cooperative Program. Each individual

Every SBC church, large or small, is completely autonomous with no directive or supervisory authority beyond the local congregation.

congregation determines the amount of its contributions to CP every year. There is not a contract, a minimum, or a guarantee other than normal budget projection processes that tell the state conventions, the SBC, or its entities how much money will be received from SBC churches and disbursed by the Cooperative Program each year. Giving to Southern Baptist Convention ministries is required for churches who send messengers to the annual meeting of the Convention. This was commonly understood to refer to Cooperative Program giving, although that was not technically necessary.

In 1925, the Convention responded to the theological controversies roiling American Christianity at the time by creating a confession of faith (also called a doctrinal statement) entitled *The Baptist Faith and Message*. This document functions as a guideline on what many Southern Baptists believe. The statement was revised by the Convention in 1963 and again in 2000. Today that statement is known as *The Baptist Faith and Message 2000*. Member churches are expected to be in friendly support of the doctrinal guidelines, and SBC seminaries are expected to employ professors who teach within its parameters. The statement does allow for some theological diversity in the SBC. It is often said that wherever you have four Baptists, you are likely to have six opinions. However, Southern Baptists take the Bible and the fundamentals of the faith quite seriously.

Churches advocating theological positions outside the common ground expressed in *The Baptist Faith and Message 2000* do not have to be accepted as member churches or seated as messengers. Membership is a voluntary association for both parties, and both must agree for that association to happen.

Through the years, the SBC became highly skilled at mobilizing its churches for missions and ministry. Thousands of local SBC churches worked together in various ministries and projects when they chose to do so, and suffered no penalty or consequences when they chose not to do so. The Convention and its churches have internal lines of authority within each church, convention, and entity, but no external directional or supervisory lines of authority. No single person or group is in charge of the Southern Baptist Convention, its entities, or its churches. All function both independently and in voluntary cooperation. In reality, SBC life is even more complicated than the brief description above, but this summary gives the reader unfamiliar with Southern Baptist polity some idea of the distinctive nature of the SBC. The working out of this plan year after year is a bit of a mystery to observe, but the model is generally reliable and productive enough to have made the SBC the nation's largest Protestant family of churches and a major influence in worldwide Christianity for many years.

Charles S. Kelley Jr.

What Do Southern Baptists Do?

In addition to the ministry of each SBC church, Southern Baptists work together in several specific ways. Their historic focus is on missions through a North American Mission Board and an International Mission Board, theological education through six seminaries, and the voicing of a Baptist perspective on national and cultural issues through the Ethics and Religious Liberty Commission. SBC churches also cooperate together in other ministry projects, including a massive ongoing ministry of disaster relief. They are widely known as the group that usually arrives first on the scene following catastrophic events, often wearing distinctive yellow hats and shirts. From time to time in its annual meeting, the Southern Baptist Convention will approve new major initiatives to mobilize its churches to accomplish big goals or institute dramatic change. Participation in such initiatives is always voluntary. The working out of these major initiatives is necessarily complicated by the unique structure and practices of the SBC.

One result of the complexities of Southern Baptist life is that even large initiatives rarely get a second glance, much less a formal evaluation, by the SBC after they are approved, unless such initiatives are connected to one or more entities or pre-existing ongoing programs. Even if a written progress or outcome report is made beyond the first year of an initiative, the effort normally receives little or no attention in the proceedings of the Convention.

The Convention is like a roaring river that keeps rushing on to the next issue without the interest or means to ask: "What happened with that last initiative?" Typically, a new SBC President is elected every two years. Knowing that he only has two years of leadership, that next President wants the SBC spotlight on the future he envisions rather than on the past and what those who went before envisioned. The *de facto* attitude of the SBC has become "If we voted approval for it, then it must have happened." A standard process for assessing the reality of what actually happens is present in SBC entities, but only rarely for the Convention as a whole.

The report that follows is in part an effort to encourage a culture of assessment in the Southern Baptist Convention by asking what actually happened after the Convention clearly decided to act. The particular subject for this assessment is the Great Commission Resurgence proposals adopted by messengers to the 2010 meeting of the SBC. In 2009, the Convention gave SBC President Johnny Hunt permission to appoint a task force to explore how to bring about a resurgence of Great Commission focus and activity in Southern Baptist life.

The Great Commission is the label commonly given to words Jesus spoke in Matthew 28:18-20
and is frequently used by evangelical Christians to
describe the task Jesus gave His disciples following
His resurrection:

> And Jesus came and spoke to them saying "All
> authority has been given to Me in heaven and on
> earth. Go therefore and make disciples of all the
> nations, baptizing them in the name of the Father
> and of the Son and of the Holy Spirit, teaching
> them to observe all things that I have command-
> ed you; and lo, I am with you always, even to the
> end of the age" Amen. (Matthew 28:18-20 NKJV).

President Hunt appointed 23 men and women
to the task force, and the Great Commission Resurgence Task Force (GCR) presented its proposed plan
to messengers in Orlando, FL at the 2010 annual
meeting. After a discussion of unusual length, the
proposals were approved by the messengers. A decade has now passed since the action of the Convention. As Winston Churchill reportedly said: "However beautiful the strategy, you should occasionally
look at the results." This project is a look at the results of how the GCR recommendations affected the
SBC in the ten years following their approval.

Be aware of what this report is and is not. It is
not a personnel evaluation, assessing the perfor-

A decade has now passed since the action of the Convention. As Winston Churchill reportedly said: "However beautiful the strategy, you should occasionally look at the results."

mance of specific people involved in the GCR process. Without question, all of them love Jesus and Southern Baptists and have accomplished great Kingdom good in their ministries. This report is an assessment of the outcomes of a strategy. What was the strategy proposed to the Southern Baptist Convention under the umbrella of a Great Commission Resurgence? What have been the results of the strategy? Can we learn anything from the GCR strategy about how to structure future SBC initiatives?

Preparing such an assessment may seem unusual to many in the Southern Baptist world, but it is standard procedure to those in the academic world. Some form of assessment process for key initiatives is required of all accredited colleges, universities, and seminaries. The typical unit of measure for such educational assessments is ten years. With this report, I am bringing to my study of Southern Baptist evangelism an informal version of a tool I spent my adult life utilizing at New Orleans Baptist Theological Seminary. Hopefully, this evaluation will not be the last attempt at an assessment of major SBC initiatives. There is much in the story of SBC initiatives that doctoral students or their professors could explore in detail to add to our understanding of Southern Baptist life and perhaps provide further insight on how to unleash the full potential of the SBC through future actions of the Convention. Having seen how little assessment has been attempted in the aftermath of major SBC initiatives, I would suggest that this topic is worthy of discussion by the SBC Executive Committee, the only entity positioned in Baptist polity to follow up Convention initiatives with five and ten-year reports of what happened after messengers approved a major initiative. I believe messengers to the SBC and others would find such information both useful and interesting.

Two important caveats must be mentioned. First, this assessment was done without the benefit of access to most of the internal documents of the GCR Task Force. Upon completing its work, the GCR Task Force decided to seal all of its documents and records for fifteen years after the proposals were presented (until 2025). This step was very unusual but not entirely unprecedented. The Peace Committee appointed during the Conservative Resurgence to deal with the complex and explosive theological issues of that day took a similar step, but the seal on their documents only lasted ten years. Eyebrows were raised at the time, but then again, they were dealing with the biggest controversy in the history of the SBC.

For the GCR Task Force to seal their documents for a much longer fifteen-year period does make one wonder what is being kept from the light of day, especially when their assignment was far less controversial than that of the Peace Committee. In my research, however, I did find at least some of the GCR documents in places that were not sealed. For example, the Task Force asked Convention attorney Jim Guenther to submit a paper on how the SBC Executive Committee could be eliminated and what the consequences would be if it were. Dr. Ed Stetzer was commissioned to write a paper on how to "unleash the North American Mission Board." Dr. David Hankins presented a paper on the perspectives of state conventions about changes in their relationships with the North American Mission Board. What other reports were prepared for the task force is unknown at this time and will be until the task force documents are unsealed.

Second, the assessment involved interactions with several of the SBC entities. With one notable exception, all were very gracious and helpful. I am indebted to the wonderful folks who work out of the spotlight in research and data collection for our entities. I wish more Southern Baptists knew of them and their work. The lone exception will be noted in the course of the assessment. Fortunately, most SBC entities have been quite transparent.

Throughout its history, the Southern Baptist Convention collected and published the basic data on what happened in the churches and entities of the Convention each year. The Annual of the Southern Baptist Convention always includes a data profile of the SBC and its entities, annual reports from each entity to Convention messengers, the proceedings of Convention business sessions, and more. Every edition of the SBC annual is now available online through the Southern Baptist Historical Library and Archives (www.sbhla.org). Dr. Taffy Hall and her team at the Archives offer invaluable assistance to any and all who are interested in learning about the history of the SBC, its entities, state conventions, and churches. This writer is deeply in their debt for help with this project.

For the GCR Task Force to seal their documents for a much longer fifteen-year period does make one wonder what is being kept from the light of day, especially when their assignment was far less controversial than that of the Peace Committee.

Prelude to the Great Commission Resurgence

The election of Adrian Rogers, pastor of Bellevue Baptist Church, to the presidency of the Southern Baptist Convention in June 1979 was a shot heard around the Southern Baptist world. His election is identified now as the official beginning of what came to be called the Conservative Resurgence, a grassroots movement calling for Southern Baptists to get re-engaged with Convention processes in order to reverse the liberal drift of the SBC. In the sixties and seventies, a movement to the theological left happened in many SBC seminaries and entities. The professional class of the SBC was increasingly out of step with Baptists in the pews and had become much more influential on the direction of the Convention than the vast majority of local churches. Concerned Southern Baptists organized a grassroots movement among those churches to get them engaged as messengers at the annual meeting in order to return the Convention to its historic theological foundations. With each passing year of the Conservative Resurgence, more and more Southern Baptists became re-engaged, pushing Convention attendance to undreamed of levels. New technology had to be invented to facilitate the involvement of more than 40,000 people, each with a voice and a vote, in a "live" business meeting that included reports, motions, and discussions open to all who were present. In the decade that followed the election of Rogers, SBC churches and their messengers made it very clear through the officers they elected and the Trustee appointments they approved that they wanted SBC leaders, professors, and workers to reflect the conservative theology and biblical values that characterized the majority of SBC churches, particularly in regard to the divine inspiration and inerrancy of the Bible.

The impact of the Conservative Resurgence was profound, bringing new trustees and presidents to every SBC entity, new faculty members to every seminary, and a fresh revision of the SBC doctrinal confession, the Baptist Faith and Message. To this day the Conservative Resurgence remains the most transformational movement in the history of the SBC. Details on this amazing chapter in the Southern Baptist story can be found in books such as *The Southern Baptist Reformation* by Jerry Sutton, *A Hill on Which to Die* by Paul Pressler and *The Conservative Resurgence in the Southern Baptist Convention* by James Hefley. The Conservative Resurgence was not an initiative formally adopted at the SBC annual meetings. It was messenger-driven rather than platform-driven. The name Conservative Resurgence came after the movement began and was used to describe what was already happening in the Convention.

The basic strategy of the Resurgence was to use the appointive powers of the SBC presidency to put people who would advocate biblical inerrancy and traditional Baptist theology in place. Those appointees would then be expected to drive the necessary change in theological direction with the internal force of Trustees and new entity leaders rather than external force from the Convention itself. Given the Baptist principle of autonomy, the use of internal force to drive change seemed to be the only appropriate path forward to those leading the Conservative Resurgence. For the first time in SBC history, consecutive SBC presidents followed the same agenda and shared goals for nearly two decades as a result of this strategic approach to change.

To this day the Conservative Resurgence remains the most transformational movement in the history of the SBC.

As the Resurgence achieved its objectives of putting entity leaders and Trustees in place, and the expected change of theological direction in the SBC occurred, attendance at the annual meeting began to decline. The huge number of newly engaged messengers appeared to assume the future of the SBC would be secure in the hands of newly installed Convention leaders. Unfortunately, a new trend not seen before in the history of the SBC began to emerge. SBC churches were becoming less fruitful, in many cases dramatically less fruitful. As the SBC started more and more new churches, the typical SBC church was baptizing fewer and fewer people. The first decade of the new millennium found a clearly conservative Southern Baptist Convention slowly becoming the Smaller Baptist Convention. Declining baptisms became the new norm. Awareness of evangelistic decline and conversations on how to address the problem slowly increased. Some specific actions were taken, but nothing showed signs of slowing the decline. As time passed, the trend towards decline spread to nearly every statistical category measured annually by the Convention (see *The Dilemma of Decline* by Charles Kelley).

At the 2008 meeting of the Southern Baptist Convention, then North American Mission Board President Geoffery Hammond announced the upcoming launch of a national evangelism initiative that would be the largest, longest, and most carefully planned effort in

The first decade of the new millennium found a clearly conservative Southern Baptist Convention slowly becoming the Smaller Baptist Convention.

SBC history to mobilize Southern Baptists to share the Gospel with every person in North America. Great Commission activities were to be undertaken on a scale never before attempted. Hammond told the 2008 messengers of his prayer that this initiative planned by representatives of national entities, state conventions, associations, and church leaders from across the country would lead to a "Great Commission Resurgence" (2008 SBC Annual, p. 184). This strategy appears to be the first instance of an effort to use the overwhelming success of the Conservative Resurgence as the backdrop for a new major initiative to revitalize the role of the Great Commission in SBC life.

In the days that followed, however, everything changed. Hammond stepped down from his leadership of NAMB in August 2009 shortly after the official launch of the *God's Plan for Sharing* initiative he hoped would spark a Great Commission Resurgence. Georgia pastor Johnny Hunt had been elected as the new SBC president at the 2008 Convention. In 2009, President Hunt decided to approach the challenge of reigniting the interest of Southern Baptists in the Great Commission in a completely different way. Ignoring Hammond's initiative, Hunt appointed a task force called the Great Commission Resurgence Task Force (GCR). That task force focused on Convention-driven initiatives rather than church-based initiatives. Shortly after the GCR approval at the 2010 Convention, a new administration began at NAMB, fully committed to implementing the new direction. The newly-launched, massive evangelism initiative jointly planned by a cross section of SBC partners quickly became a footnote in SBC history. With the clarity hindsight always brings, one can say the year between the 2009 and the 2010 Convention meetings turned out to be a hinge that opened the door to a very different chapter in the SBC story.

Birth of the Great Commission Resurgence

In a chapel message on April 16, 2009, Daniel Akin, president of Southeastern Baptist Theological Seminary, used Hammond's term "Great Commission Resurgence" but defined it in a completely different way. He suggested twelve axioms that would be necessary for a Great Commission Resurgence. Those twelve axioms were:

1. We must commit ourselves to the total and absolute Lordship of Jesus Christ in every area of our lives.
2. We must be gospel-centered in all our endeavors for the glory of God.
3. We must take our stand on the firm foundation of the inerrant and infallible Word of God affirming its sufficiency in all matters.
4. We must devote ourselves to a radical pursuit of the Great Commission in the context of obeying the Great Commandments.

5. We must affirm the *Baptist Faith and Message 2000* as a healthy and sufficient guide for building a theological consensus for partnership in the gospel, refusing to be sidetracked by theological agendas that distract us from our Lord's Commission

6. We must dedicate ourselves to a passionate pursuit of the Great Commission of the Lord Jesus across our nation and to all nations answering the call to go, disciple, baptize, and teach all that the Lord commanded.

7. We must covenant to build gospel saturated homes that see children as a gift from God and as our first and primary mission field.

8. We must recognize the need to rethink our Convention structure and identity so that we maximize our energy and resources for the fulfilling of the Great Commission.

9. We must see the necessity for pastors to be faithful Bible preachers who teach us both the content of the Scriptures and the theology embedded in the Scriptures.

10. We must encourage pastors to see themselves as the head of a gospel missions agency who will lead the way in calling out the called for international assignments but also equip and train all their people to see themselves as missionaries for Jesus regardless of where they live.

11. We must pledge ourselves to a renewed cooperation that is gospel-centered and built around a biblical and theological core and not methodological consensus or agreement.

12. We must accept our constant need to humble ourselves and repent of pride, arrogance, jealousy, hatred, contentions, lying, selfish ambitions, laziness, complacency, idolatries, and other sins of the flesh; pleading with our Lord to do what only He can do in us and through us and all for His glory.

SBC President Hunt resonated with the proposals recommended by Akin, and he decided to make this approach to a Great Commission Resurgence the centerpiece of his presidency.

Arrangements were made for R. Albert Mohler, president of the Southern Baptist Theological Seminary, to make a motion at the 2009 Convention meeting in Louisville that the SBC grant the president the authority to appoint a task force to prepare proposals for actions that would result in a Great Commission Resurgence among Southern Baptists. The resulting group of 23 Southern Baptists was scheduled to make its report and recommend proposals for consideration at the 2010 meeting of the SBC.

The appointment of a Great Commission Resurgence Task Force aroused immediate attention across the SBC. The clear implication in the name of the task force was that the intended goal was to create a Great Commission impact comparable to the massive theological impact of the Conservative Resurgence that had so deeply transformed the Convention in earlier years. To accomplish this objective, proponents chose a very different strategy, going with a top-down approach rather than the grassroots approach of the Conservative Resurgence. As reports on the work of the task force began to circulate, the early indications were that adjustments to the fund-raising and distribution process of the Convention and altering the historic relationships between the state conventions and the North American Mission Board were priorities of the task force rather than mobilizing and enabling local churches to reach their communities for Christ, as envisioned in the *God's Plan for Sharing* initiative. This focus on structural changes and funding changes came in spite of the massive restructuring process the Convention underwent only fifteen years earlier in the Covenant for a New Century (*1995 SBC Annual*, pp. 151-176).

> *To accomplish this objective, proponents chose a very different strategy, going with a top-down approach rather than the grass-roots approach of the Conservative Resurgence.*

In June 2010, the North American Mission Board announced to the SBC the formal launch of *God's Plan for Sharing* to mobilize Southern Baptists for a decade of evangelism. At the same Convention, the Great Commission Task Force brought its final report to the messengers. Following extended and at times heated discussion, the GCR proposals were approved. No comments were made nor were questions asked about any relationship between the two reports during business sessions. The full report of the task force to the Convention and the record of the discussion and votes are found in the 2010 *Annual of the Southern Baptist Convention*, p. 78ff. All annuals of the SBC are available online in the digital resources section of the website of the Southern Baptist Historical Library and Archives (www.sbhla.org).

The messengers appeared to perceive that money was at the heart of the GCR proposals and the SBC funding process was the area most likely to change if the proposals were adopted. Several attempts were made to table or refer the proposals for further study, but all failed. Most of the discussion centered on the proposal to create a new giving category to be recognized apart from the Cooperative Program. After several votes and heated discussions on the Great Commission Giving language, an effort was made to amend the language that was a clear concern for many of the messengers. Eventually the task force and the messenger proposing amended language reached a compromise in a "back room" negotiation on the platform. Messengers approved the compromise amendment, and the GCR proposals were adopted as the time for discussion expired. The time given to the discussion on the Great Commission Giving language meant very little else about the GCR proposals was discussed by the messengers.

The passing of a decade since the 2010 approval offers an excellent context for an outcomes assessment of the Great Commission Resurgence proposals. Factors beyond the control of the Southern Baptist Convention always affect SBC churches, such as cultural change, economic turmoil, the rise of Reformed theology, etc. Such factors are beyond the scope of this assessment. The GCR was a specific action taken by the Convention with a specific outcome in mind. Thus, the essential question of this assessment: Are there now signs of a Great Commission Resurgence among the churches of the SBC as a result of the Great Commission Resurgence proposals implemented following their approval in 2010?

Part Two:

The Great Commission Resurgence Proposals

Task Force Chair Dr. Ronnie Floyd chose to bundle all of the GCR proposals into a single motion for consideration and approval by the Convention. The various proposals were grouped under one of seven Components. Those Components were further distilled into seven specific recommendations comprising a single motion for approval by SBC messengers. Each Component and its proposals will be identified and examined in light of its results after a decade.

Charles S. Kelley Jr.

Component One: Getting the Mission Right

The purpose of this component was to create a permanent mission statement for the SBC. Given the nature of the Convention as an unusual type of organization, such a statement was destined to be ignored.

> *As a convention of churches, our missional vision is to present the Gospel of Jesus Christ to every person in the world and to make disciples of all the nations (2010 SBC Annual, p. 81).*

The concept of a mission statement and the language used in the one proposed incorporated fairly traditional terminology widely understood and accepted by most Southern Baptists. Some might think it unusual that it did not include the simple words of Jesus in the Great Commission on how to measure progress towards accomplishing the mission: the baptism of converts and their instruction in His teachings (Matt. 28:19-20). This omission was not viewed as controversial by messengers, probably in light of the long familiarity with and popularity of the Great Commission in SBC life. The proposal was approved without question.

WHAT HAPPENED?

In the decade since its approval, the mission statement virtually disappeared almost immediately, remaining largely ignored and unused, having no noticeable place in or measurable effect on the Convention and its churches. The mission statement has not been published in the Annual of the Southern Baptist Convention, the SBC Business and Financial Plan, or in the daily Bulletins at the annual meetings of the SBC. It was not included in the reports of the Executive Committee to the Convention, nor was it referenced in the more than thirty Executive Committee meetings this writer attended after its adoption. The statement is not included in the documents of any SBC entity or posted in a significant place in the SBC building in Nashville. Any references to it by SBC presidents or entity leaders are rare and infrequent at best. The lack of attention is not the result of opposition or controversy of any sort. Just the opposite. A formal mission statement is largely irrelevant to an SBC that operates as a voluntary organization of autonomous churches and entities. The SBC neither directs nor evaluates the actions, ministries, or personnel of its member churches or entities. Many of those autonomous churches and entities have their own mission statements. In the rhythms of SBC life, there is no clear and obvious place for a mission statement to be repeated, explained, or applied.

Mission statements emerged in the life of corporate America many years ago as a tool to keep organizations focused on why they exist and to help them avoid being distracted by pursuits that may be interesting but are irrelevant to the purpose of the corporation or business. From corporate America the use of mission statements began to migrate into SBC churches and ministries with that same purpose, as a way to keep a church or ministry focused on why it exists and to protect against distraction by matters of lesser importance. For a mission statement to work as a device to focus an organization, it has to be continually promoted and reviewed so that everyone knows and understands it, and it has to be consistently applied in the decision-making and evaluation process of the organization. The stability and constant interactivity of a corporation, a business, a church, or a specific ministry can build

In the decade since its approval, the mission statement virtually disappeared almost immediately, remaining largely ignored and unused, having no noticeable place in or measurable effect on the Convention and its churches.

The SBC neither directs nor evaluates the actions, ministries, or personnel of its member churches or entities.

31

that continual review and consistent application process into the way things work so that everyone connected to the organization comes to know and be guided by the statement.

Unlike many organizations, the Southern Baptist Convention only exists for two days each year. The composition of the messengers forming the Convention is different every year. There is a different president every year or two. All SBC churches are autonomous, meaning they determine themselves their mission and how they want to operate. There is no vehicle to review an SBC mission statement continually so that all churches and their members understand it and use it. There is no obvious means to apply it frequently enough for it to become accepted and useful in SBC processes. Motions or resolutions from a messenger may be ruled in order or out of order on the basis of SBC By-laws or Robert's Rules of Order. They are never ruled irrelevant to the mission of the Convention. The task force recommended a mission statement but did not include any recommendations on where or how the mission statement would be published or used. This was a mission statement in a vacuum preserved for posterity but not for use.

The only possible place for an SBC mission statement to be consistently reviewed and applied in decision making is in the Executive Committee of the SBC, which operates on behalf of the Convention between meetings of the Convention. When the

Executive Committee failed to incorporate the use of the mission statement in its ongoing processes to do the business of either the Executive Committee or the Convention, the statement was bound to disappear. Two GCR Task Force members eventually served as Executive Committee president, but they also ignored the SBC mission statement. The missional statement proved to be more window dressing for the moment than a useful tool. Nothing was lost by adopting the missional statement, but neither was anything gained.

The missional statement proved to be more window dressing for the moment than a useful tool.

Component Two: Making Our Values Transparent

The purpose of this component was to provide values to be used as guidelines by the Convention as it engaged in its business and its ministries. As was true with the vision statement, the unusual nature of the Convention as an organization rendered the value statement largely irrelevant in the context of the Convention. This was an action without a consequence.

> We call upon Southern Baptists to embrace and adopt these Core Values as a means of ensuring that we work together in a way that will please our Lord and reflect our identity as fellow believers in service to the Lord Jesus Christ (*2010 SBC Annual*, p. 82).

a. Christ-Likeness
b. Truth
c. Unity
d. Relationships
e. Trust
f. Future

g. Local Church
h. Kingdom

These are traditional biblical values expressed in common language often used among Southern Baptists, needing little definition, elaboration, or defense. They were approved without discussion.

As was the case with the mission statement, references to these core values have been extremely rare since the approval vote. They are not controversial. There has been no movement to amend or replace them. The Convention is not the kind of organization that functions in a way that allows formal core values to influence how it conducts business. The core values that most affect the Convention are the ones the messengers already have and bring to the annual meeting from their churches and their personal lives. There is no forum for teaching or explaining these core values to Southern Baptists on any sort of regular basis. As noted earlier, the Convention only exists for two days every year. Every year different messengers compose the Convention, and every other year a different President leads the Convention. There is no mechanism to continually and consistently promote the core values among the 48,000 churches of the SBC.

The Southern Baptist Convention was not created to shape and mold the attitudes of its messengers and churches because each church is autonomous and functions as it pleases. The Convention was created to mobilize SBC churches for the work of the Great Commission to reach the nation and the world for Christ. Pastors and lay leaders do not look to the SBC for guidance in how to behave. Sermons, resolutions, or speeches addressing the behavior of churches, messengers, or churches do come from the platform from time to time, but such efforts are incidental or supplementary to the primary mission and focus of the Convention. Those that have any traction beyond a particular Convention are more a reflection of what concerns SBC churches at the moment than marching orders to churches awaiting instruction. The preeminent concern of typical Southern Baptists is what can be done to maximize their impact in fulfilling the Great Commission. A study of the aftermath of Convention actions addressing behavior specifically would be an interesting and useful study, but it

The Southern Baptist Convention was not created to shape and mold the attitudes of its messengers and churches because each church is autonomous and functions as it pleases. The Convention was created to mobilize SBC churches for the work of the Great Commission to reach the nation and the world for Christ.

is not the purpose of this study. The Executive Committee, which does exist continually and could focus on such things, chose not to incorporate the values into their processes or their publications. The recommended core values have not been consistently published by the EC, promoted through the EC, nor referrenced during the business processes of the EC.

WHAT HAPPENED?

In the decade that followed the adoption of the Great Commission Resurgence proposals, the statement of Core Values has been neither a problem nor a blessing for the SBC. It was an action without a consequence due to the amorphous nature of the Southern Baptist Convention as an organization. The task force apparently envisioned the SBC as an organization that functioned like a church, when in fact it is a completely different organization whose purpose is to create a cooperative synergy out of the work of autonomous, independent churches and entities. The focus is on coordinated effort, not coordinated management.

The use of a mission statement and core values statement are classic management tools offered to Southern Baptists. However, Southern Baptist churches are looking for mobilization and coordination tools, not directive management. To use an analogy: the SBC is more like a traffic cop than the driver of a car. Each driver in traffic controls his own vehicle. The traffic cop is there to facilitate a smooth flow of vehicles together, not to operate the vehicles. Because the annual meeting of the Southern Baptist Convention is a business meeting, the classic guide to public meetings, Robert's Rules of Order and the SBC By-laws are far more important than a largely invisible and virtually unknown mission statement and core values statement. When Convention debates become very heated, the SBC President will seek to restore calm by an appeal to Robert's Rules of Order, not to the SBC values adopted with the GCR proposals.

The focus is on coordinated effort, not coordinated management.

Charles S. Kelley Jr.

Component Three: Encouraging Cooperative Program Giving and Other Great Commission Giving

Component Three generated enormous controversy and dominated virtually all discussion about GCR both before and during the Convention. Many Southern Baptists felt it was recommending a competitor to the Cooperative Program, although that was denied by the task force. The celebration and praise of designated giving was the root of the controversy. By the time discussion on this component was finished, no time was left for messengers to discuss the remaining proposals.

> *We call upon Southern Baptists to honor and affirm the Cooperative Program as the most effective means of mobilizing our churches and extending our reach. We also call upon Southern Baptists to celebrate all giving to our common work. We will recognize the total of all monies channeled through the causes of the Southern Baptist Convention, the state conventions and associations, as Great Commission Giving.*

The Best Intentions

We call upon Southern Baptists to adopt goals of giving no less than $200 million annually through the Lottie Moon Christmas Offering for International Missions and $100 million annually through the Annie Armstrong Easter Offering for North American Missions by 2015.

We call upon the churches to increase the percentage of their Cooperative Program giving.

We call upon the state conventions to increase the percentage of Cooperative Program funds directed to the Southern Baptist Convention.

We call upon every entity of the Southern Baptist Convention to maximize all Cooperative Program funds for the task of taking the Gospel to the nations and serving Great Commission churches in their fulfillment of this mandate.

We call all Southern Baptists to incorporate planned gifts supporting the Great Commission into their estate planning.

We call upon all Southern Baptists to celebrate every dollar given by faithful Southern Baptists as part of Great Commission Giving, including designated gifts given to any Baptist association or state convention, and to all causes of the Southern Baptist Convention.

We call upon all Southern Baptists to evaluate every budget, personal and Convention-related, in terms of a Great Commission focus and commitment (2010 SBC Annual, pp. 82-83).

Many Southern Baptists felt that Great Commission Giving was the heart of the GCR proposals because it generated a great deal of comment and discussion before, during, and after the Convention. Great Commission Giving alone absorbed nearly all of the time for discussion of the whole GCR proposal during the Convention. Component Three is actually the first Component to include a collection of proposals bundled together to present as a group. The purpose of all items included in the collection was to make significant adjustments to the funding process of the SBC, both fund-raising and funding distribution.

The first part of the proposal affirmed the crucial role of the Cooperative Program for funding SBC efforts to fulfill the Great Commission. However, for the first time in the history of major SBC proposals, the task force chose not to emphasize the exclusive promotion of the Cooperative Program and the two annual mission offerings as the Southern Baptist way to fund the Great Commission. The Task Force also called for the creation of a new category for designated giving that goes around the CP process. This new category would be called Great Commission Giving and would include designated giving to all Southern Baptist causes. The official definition of Great Commission Giving from the Executive Committee is "the total amount of all money given to Southern Baptist mission causes by SBC congregations including Cooperative Program, Annie Armstrong, and Lottie Moon, plus monies given to associations, state conventions (such as a state mission offering), and any other Southern Baptist mission cause." In the words of the Task Force Report:

> *We also call upon Southern Baptists to celebrate all giving to our common work. We will recognize the total of all monies channeled through the causes of the Southern Baptist Convention, the state conventions, and associations as Great Commission Giving* (2010 *SBC Annual*, p. 82).

The only thing more controversial the Task Force could have done related to SBC missions and evangelism would have been to recommend eliminating the Cooperative Program. More than the creation of a new giving category, the apparent intent was to give designated giving the same level of recognition and celebration across the SBC as giving to the Cooperative Program. In other words, they

However, for the first time in the history of major SBC proposals, the task force chose not to emphasize the exclusive promotion of the Cooperative Program and the two annual mission offerings as the Southern Baptist way to fund the Great Commission.

created a package for the promotion and praise of designated giving by SBC churches. This moved designated giving from the background of SBC life to center stage, sharing the spotlight with the

Great Commission Giving was not intended to introduce a new way for Southern Baptist churches to give, but it was a new way for SBC churches and their pastors to be recognized, praised, and celebrated in the Convention for their giving.

Cooperative Program. Any SBC leader would have known the introduction of a *de facto* competitor to CP would create an uproar. Apparently, the Task Force was so committed to this proposal that they were willing to shift the Convention's attention away from the emerging evangelism crisis in the churches and make the SBC funding process the primary focus of Convention attention. They were very willing to unleash the resulting controversy.

Great Commission Giving was not intended to introduce a new way for Southern Baptist churches to give, but it was a new way for SBC churches and their pastors to be recognized, praised, and celebrated in the Convention for their giving.

The role of low self-esteem in the contemporary SBC may be the most overlooked issue in the crises facing today's Convention. A further discussion of this point is beyond the scope of this assess-

The role of low self-esteem in the contemporary SBC may be the most overlooked issue in the crises facing today's Convention.

ment, but the issue does appear to be a factor in SBC life worth watching.

Southern Baptists were called upon and encouraged to support and participate in Cooperative Program giving to some extent. By contrast, however, in three different sections of Component Three, Southern Baptists were called upon to celebrate (praise, recognize, affirm) Great Commission Giving.

As noted earlier, this part of the proposal created quite a stir among Southern Baptists across the Convention before the Orlando meeting, and the discussion of it absorbed most of the time and energy for the discussion of the whole report when it was put before the messengers. In fact, it very nearly shut down the approval process for the whole proposal. The deep concern was driven by the fear of undermining support for the Cooperative Program, universally recognized as the financial lifeblood of the SBC. Motions to amend the language on Great Commission Giving began as soon as the Convention floor was open for new business, before the report was formally presented to messengers. When the report was finally placed before the messengers for action, an amendment to eliminate all the language about Great Commission Giving, leaving only the language affirming the Cooperative Program in place made it to the floor for consideration. After much discussion and a time of prayer about the pending decision (a very unusual step), a vote was taken in the normal way by raised ballots. The Chair ruled the results too close to call from the platform, meaning a ballot vote would have to take place. The approval process for the whole report was about to be disrupted and put at risk.

Before the ballot vote could be taken, Task Force Chairman Ronnie Floyd asked for a very rare timeout in the midst of the discussion in order to attempt to cut a deal with the messenger who proposed the amendment. The pause was granted by President Hunt, and in a private conversation on the platform while messengers watched and wondered, Floyd offered to add stronger language affirming the Cooperative Program if the language about Great Commission Giving was allowed to remain. The messenger agreed to the compromise, and the amendment as proposed in the compromise passed a raised ballot vote.

Much about the determination of the task force to introduce intentionally such strong controversy into their proposals is unknown. Here is what is known. The families of churches (denominations) that comprise American Christianity all have ministries and missions outside of their local churches that require financial support from their churches in order to accomplish their assigned task. Virtually all other denominations support their joint ministry projects and missions through some form of designated giving. In many denominations, congregations have an assigned amount to give per church that goes to the denomination as a form of dues for belonging. Churches and church members can provide financial support outside of the assigned amount for the denomination and ignore everything else. Others have ministry connections based on fundraising in congregations. Whoever can get fundraisers in churches and on the financial radar of church members usually wins. Whoever does not succeed in arousing passion for their cause, loses. In 1925 Southern Baptists decided to take a very different approach. Rather than the fundraisers for joint SBC ministries competing to get into churches and connected to church budgets, Southern Baptists created a common pot from which all state, national, and international joint ministries would be funded. That common pot was called the Cooperative Program. In response to support from the Cooperative Program, any SBC entity or ministry benefitting from CP was not allowed to go to individual churches and fund-raise for their particular ministries. This plan reduced the pressure on local churches to do special offerings or fund-raising drives for ministries outside of the local church, allowing space to promote all SBC ministries through the common purse of CP.

Every Southern Baptist church is encouraged to put any amount of money it chooses into that common pot. Each state convention of SBC churches promotes CP and serves as the collecting point to receive funds for the Cooperative Program. Each state convention determines how much of the Cooperative Program to keep for the joint ministries of churches in the state and how much to send on to the national SBC for joint ministries of all Southern Baptists across the nation and the world. Formulas for the distribution of those funds are created by each state convention and the national Southern Baptist Convention. Those formulas must be approved by messengers who attend the various conventions on behalf of the participating churches. Although the SBC is composed primarily of small churches (about 70% have fewer than 100 people in attendance; about 90% have fewer than 250), the amount of money raised annually through the Cooperative Program and the stability of that funding for such a wide variety of joint ministry projects typically exceeds the designated giving approach of other denominations. Gifts to the Cooperative Program help and strengthen every joint ministry in the state, the nation, and the world, giving thousands of smaller churches an opportunity to have a true worldwide impact. Designated giving just helps one ministry at a time.

One critical reason for the success of the Cooperative Program is its seamless connection to a very organized designated giving strategy for the two most popular recipients of CP funding. A special offering for the International Mission Board (Lottie Moon) and a special offering for the North American Mission Board

Gifts to the Cooperative Program help and strengthen every joint ministry in the state, the nation, and the world, giving thousands of smaller churches an opportunity to have a true worldwide impact. Designated giving just helps one ministry at a time.

(Annie Armstrong) are collected each year. Both are quite popular and supported by the vast majority of SBC churches. Southern Baptists never connect the dots in this way, but the annual offerings are in effect a designated giving channel allowing churches and individuals that particularly want to give most of their money exclusively to missions can do so with the full blessing of the Convention CP protocols. Each mission offering dramatically increases the funding of the mission boards, but in a way that does not take away or detract from the funding of all SBC ministries through the Cooperative Program. Time proved this fund-raising paradigm to be a work of genius, incorporating an element of designated giving into a funding process in which every dollar given to the Cooperative Program is spread among the many state, national, and international ministries of the SBC. As this writer talked to leaders in other denominations through the years, they consistently indicated amazement and envy at how well this distinctive approach has worked in providing stable, significant support for all SBC ministries. As the president of a Catholic university said after hearing how CP works: "Where can I sign up to be a Baptist?"

The passing years demonstrated the power of the Cooperative Program model. A natural result was the Convention's affirmation of churches and pastors who supported it. An ideal level of CP support for a church came to be viewed by many as ten percent or more of a church's budget. For many in SBC life the percentage of support from a church's budget was noticed more than the dollar amount given, perhaps because the typical SBC church is smaller. For years, those who led in the SBC tended to come from the ranks of those who were clear supporters of the Cooperative Program. Then came the Conservative Resurgence, mentioned at the beginning of this assessment. Most of the messengers who attended the SBC meetings and cast the votes that made the Conservative Resurgence possible came from the smaller churches that were typical of the SBC. The high-profile pastoral leaders who "rallied the troops" to come to Conventions for the Resurgence and were elected as SBC presidents tended to be from larger churches who often did not have track records of significant CP support. Messengers in those days were willing to overlook the tepid support of CP by candidates put forward during the Conservative Resurgence in order to change the theological direction of the SBC. The crisis of liberalism was a more immediate crisis than speeding the growth of CP. Still, the need to change the theological direction of the Convention did not squelch the criticism of those who were in SBC leadership but were not actively supporting the Cooperative Program.

Again and again, conservative, large church pastors given leadership positions in the SBC were criticized for only token support of the Cooperative Program. When two megachurch pastors giving only marginal support to both CP and the two SBC mission offerings were chosen to lead the two mission boards, such criticisms became even more pronounced. Pastors in the designated giving tradition would often point to the large amounts of money given to a variety of mission causes, but critics would say, such designated giving was not the Southern Baptist way. When pastors of very large churches would point to the dollar amount of their gifts to CP, others would say the percentage of CP giving was a clearer reflection of the true level of support for the joint ministries of Southern Baptists. The tensions between those committed to the Cooperative

Program strategy and those preferring designated giving and/or total dollars given to CP versus percentages of a budget as the primary means of mission support continued to grow. Not being publicly recognized and praised for the large dollar amounts given, even if the percentage of their church budgets was small, "stuck in the craw" of many pastors who preferred to focus on their designated gifts.

It is quite possible that the push to put recognition and praise for designated giving on par with giving through the systematic approach of the Cooperative Program grew out of some of these long-standing frustrations. Pastors leading their churches to emphasize a designated giving approach to SBC support wanted the same kind of public affirmation and praise as those who emphasized giving through the CP. The concern of those supporting CP was that the promotion of Great Commission Giving could have the unintended consequence of undermining the historic financial model of the SBC, a model that far exceeded the results of other denominations who emphasized designated giving to missions and ministry as their primary model.

As the Task Force considered the best way to fund the Great Commission efforts of the SBC in the 21st century, they decided to take a risk and break away from giving exclusive attention to promoting the Cooperative Program. Instead, they called upon Southern Baptists to celebrate both designated giving and the systematic support of all joint SBC ministries provided by the Cooperative Program. Great Commission Giving incorporating all giving to any SBC cause was the GCR Task Force's way to bring praise and honor to the designated giving of those not appreciated for their level of systematic CP support.

The concern of those supporting CP was that the promotion of Great Commission Giving could have the unintended consequence of undermining the historic financial model of the SBC, a model that far exceeded the results of other denominations who emphasized designated giving to missions and ministry as their primary model.

The next part of Component Three addressed the two annual offerings for the mission boards. Southern Baptists were called upon to adopt goals of no less than $200 million given annually to the Lottie Moon Christmas Offering for International Missions and $100 Million given annually through the Annie Armstrong Easter Offering for North American Missions by 2015. The International Mission Board, the North American Mission Board, and the Woman's Missionary Union (WMU) would have had to adopt those goals to make them official. Typically, WMU took the lead in announcing the annual mission offering goals. Support for these goals from those bodies was not mentioned. Apparently, they were not consulted by the Task Force prior to this public announcement. No endorsement from any of the three organizations was included with the recommendation, and such endorsements did not follow the release of the report. This writer has not found any reference to the suggested goals from any of the organizations in the decade since the proposals were adopted. To reach those goals would have required increasing the offerings by roughly $50 million in only five years. No explanation on how the Task Force settled on those goals was included with the proposal.

Great Commission Giving incorporating all giving to any SBC cause was the GCR Task Force's way to bring praise and honor to the designated giving of those not appreciated for their level of systematic CP support.

The third part of Component Three called for SBC churches to increase the percentage of their church budgets given to the Cooperative Program annually. No specific percentage was recommended as a goal for consideration. No particular benefits that would follow such action were mentioned. The Task Force did not appear to see any irony in calling for increased affirmation and celebration of designated giving by churches while at the same time calling for an increase in percentage giving to CP.

The fourth aspect of Component Three was a call for all state conventions to increase the percentage of Cooperative Program gifts being forwarded to the national Southern Baptist Convention. No target percentages or dates for making these changes were included in the proposal, nor were any benefits to the state conventions for making such changes identified. Two state convention executives served on the task force, and therefore had a voice in the preparation of this recommendation. Although the Task Force made no public reference to it, they did meet with a group of state convention executives to hear and discuss a paper addressing the role of state conventions in SBC life. That paper (Address to the Great Commission Task Force) was prepared and presented by Dr. David Hankins, then serving as state executive for the Louisiana Baptist Convention. It is included in those records that will be unsealed in fifteen years, but a copy was made available to this writer for this assessment project.

Hankins noted the absence of any formal evidence that Southern Baptists were unhappy with the existing process of CP distribution between the state conventions and the SBC. By contrast, there was specific evidence indicating satisfaction with the process as it was. Three separate surveys of Southern Baptists through the years indicated they were generally happy with the CP allocation process as it was. The last of those three surveys was a "massive" (Hankins' term) project undertaken by LifeWay Research on behalf of the SBC Executive Committee a year before the GCR task force was formed. It also affirmed wide support of the present process. In addition, Hankins noted the number of churches giving directly to the SBC to avoid the state conventions was going down, not up. The Hankins paper gave very specific numbers based on CP data. In the seven years prior to the GCR process, the total dollars given directly to the Convention dropped 30% while "standard CP giving rose over 10% in the same period." If CP giving was declining, it did not appear to be the result of widespread dissatisfaction with the distribution process between the state conventions and the SBC. Hankins further noted that all state convention allocation processes were determined by and overseen by the messengers representing the local churches in each state convention every year, not by state convention staff.

The fifth proposed action called upon Southern Baptists to engage in estate planning with the Great Commission in mind so that financial support for the Great Commission could continue after members passed on to glory. Oddly, no reference was made to the Southern Baptist Foundation or the various state convention foundations that could have helped interested Southern Baptists know how to include the Great Commission in their estate planning. This failure to make any reference to the various Southern Baptist foundations already in existence is a bit of a surprise, since all of them were created in part for just this purpose and could have provided easily accessible assistance to Southern Baptists who wanted to include some form of Great Commission support in their estate plans. No targets or goals were included.

In addition to these specific actions, Southern Baptists were called upon to evaluate all budgets–personal and ministry–in light of the Great Commission, to support the Cooperative Program and to celebrate Great Commission giving to any SBC cause. The stated purpose of all these recommendations was to increase the amount of money available for Southern Baptist churches and entities to spend on Great Commission activities and by so doing increase the number of people being reached with the Gospel.

What Happened?

Generating an enlarged income stream from SBC churches to fund increased Great Commission activity and ministry by the Southern Baptist Convention was one of the highest priorities for the GCR Task Force and the particular focus of Component Three. A decade after all of their proposals were approved, that goal is largely unmet.

After creating so much controversy before and during the 2010 Convention, Great Commission

Giving is rarely mentioned in SBC conversations to-day. The category was added to the list of annual SBC statistics but largely ignored as a measure of SBC health. According to SBC annuals, it reached a high of $777,452,820 in 2013. Since that high, it has declined for five of the last eight years. Great Commission Giving in 2019 was $540,859,296 (a decrease of more than $200 million) and $409,835,470 in the pandemic year of 2020. Some state conventions do not track Great Commission Giving or report it as a giving category. There is little evidence that the amount of Great Commission Giving by a church has become a badge of honor for a pastor.

SBC churches did not increase the percentage of their gifts to the Cooperative Program nor give to the Lottie Moon and Annie Armstrong mission offerings at the rate projected by the Task Force. The projections of $200 million for Lottie Moon and $100 million for Annie Armstrong by 2015 did not materialize, even when a crisis developed un-expectedly. Not long after the GCR proposals were passed, the International Mission Board was forced to bring missionaries home and ask for early retire-ments because they did not have the funds to sup-port the missionaries already on the field. There are no indications of any increase in the role of the Great Commission in estate planning by Southern Baptists, nor have there been any further large-scale promotions of this recommendation after the GCR proposals were adopted. The rate of fiscal growth for the Southern Baptist Convention is in a decades long trend of slowing, and that downward trend has actually accelerated since 2010.

The *Annual of the Southern Baptist Convention* is the official source of data about the SBC and its churches. The chart below, updated by the Executive Committee each year, is from SBC annuals. Percentage changes in SBC giving trends are tracked by the decade as well as year to year. Numbers in a parenthesis indicate a percentage decrease over previous years. For Southern Baptist churches, the crucial factors to note are the slowing growth of both total church receipts and the total undesignated gifts that flow into local church budgets. For the Southern Baptist Convention, the most concerning category is the percentage of undesignated gifts to churches being sent to the Cooperative Program. In nearly every category, the rate of growth in giving slows through the years, but since 2010, slowing growth turned into accelerating decline in total receipts by SBC churches and total CP gifts from SBC churches.

Not long after the GCR proposals were passed, the International Mission Board was forced to bring missionaries home and ask for early retirements because they did not have the funds to support the missionaries already on the field.

Decadal Percentage Changes in SBC Giving (1970-2021)

Years	Total Receipts by SBC Churches	Total of Undes-ignated Gifts to SBC Churches	Total CP Gifts from SBC Churches	SBC Share of Total CP	Total CP as % of Undes-ignated Gifts
1970s	9.94%	NA	8.97%	34.41%	N/A
1980s	7.58%	5.10%	6.83%	37.47%	10.50%
1990s	5.42%	4.91%	2.68%	37.04%	8.73%
2000s	4.12%	4.82%	2.23%	37.16%	6.80%
2010s	(0.21%)	0.71%	(1.16%)	39.34%	5.22%
Last 5 Yrs	0.65%	1.20%	(0.73%)	41.27%	4.79%

Chart prepared from the Southern Baptist Convention Annual of 2019 and Book of Reports, 2022.

The decade following the adoption of the Great Commission Resurgence proposals did not produce a resurgence in funding for the Great Commission. In the eighties, SBC churches were giving an average of 10.5% of their undesignated gifts to the Cooperative Program. For the last five years, they have been sending an average of 4.79% of undesignated receipts to CP. Even more concerning is the downward trend in undesignated gifts to SBC churches. In the eighties, undesignated gifts to

SBC churches increased annually at an average of 5.10%. Since the GCR proposals were adopted, the average increase has been only 0.71% annually.

There is one notable exception: the SBC share of CP has clearly increased since the GCR called for the state conventions to send on a higher percentage to the national Convention. In the first decade of the 21st century, the state conventions were sending an average of 37.16% to the national CP. For the last five years, they sent an average of 41.08%. However, the increase is in fact a larger piece of a shrinking pie. There was no corresponding growth in total gifts to CP to offset the increased percentage sent to the national CP fund for most state conventions. The ministries and services provided by state conventions to their churches had to shrink as the state conventions passed on more money to the national convention. The following chart on the pages 62-63 shows the decline in actual dollars of Cooperative Program giving which followed the Great Commission Resurgence. The percentage of money going to the SBC grew, but it was a growing percentage from a smaller pie. The final chart in the series shows the annual amount of

The decade following the adoption of the Great Commission Resurgence proposals did not produce a resurgence in funding for the Great Commission.

Great Commission Giving since the category was created by the GCR proposals. It, too, has declined.

The goals for the Lottie Moon and Annie Armstrong offerings appear to have been little more than wishful thinking. In 2010, the Lottie Moon Christmas Offering recorded gifts of 145,662,925. In 2015, the total recorded was $165,798,102. For the Annie Armstrong Offering the 2010 total was $52,415,505. In 2015 the amount received was $55,610,226. These are far from GCR projections.

The percentage of money going to the SBC grew, but it was a growing percentage from a smaller pie.

Apparently, the Task Force recommendation that Lottie Moon have not less than $200 million in receipts and Annie Armstrong have not less than $100 million by 2015 was a goal too unrealistic to embrace or even consider by the mission boards, the WMU, or the Convention. The International Mission Board, North American Mission Board and WMU ignored the recommended goals of the Task Force and continued with their existing goal setting process.

The evidence in the following chart indicates the GCR had a minimal effect on increasing Southern Baptist financial support for missions. The change in Cooperative Program distribution by state conventions gave the two mission boards a larger piece of a smaller pie, but not on a game changing scale.

As of 2021, the mission offerings are yet to approach the recommended goals for 2015. Most importantly, the number of missionaries deployed by both the International Mission Board and the North American Mission boards also significantly decreased by the end of the decade.

SBC Missions (2010 - 2021)

Year	NAMB Cooperative Program	Annie Armstrong Offering	NAMB Missionaries
2010	$43,702,822	$52,415,505	5,096
2011	$43,729,142	$54,673,399	+2,616
2012	$43,683,642	$55,472,759	2,400
2013	$42,845,490	$54,957,016	2,406
2014	$42,518,758	$55,674,122	2,178
2015	$43,109,617	$55,610,226	++5,684
2016	$44,606,983	$56,056,232	5,684
2017	$45,894,865	$55,553,453	5,262
2018	$44,849,541	$56,668,218	5,097
2019	$44,835,155	$56,260,700	+++3,057
2020	$43,962,104	$43,502,420	2,218
2021	$43,773,080	$59,148,967	2,469

Year	IMB Cooperative Program	Lottie Moon Offering	IMB Missionaries
2010	$95,881,376	$145,662,925	5,031
2011	$95,939,322	$146,828,116	4,857

2012	$96,268,287	$149,276,303	4,850
2013	$94,376,650	$154,057,852	4,815
2014	$94,048,732	$153,002,394	4,792
2015	$95,362,518	$165,798,102	3.971
2016	$98,722,209	$152,982,560	3,596
2017	$98,792,233	*$14,766,873	3,563
2018	$99,347,638	$158,865,136	3,457
2019	$99,254,130	$157,300,000	3,615
2020	$97,241,319	$123,237,630	3,558
2021	$96,823,210	$128,285,813	3,592

*A change in IMB reporting dates provides only a partial year total in 2017.

+Beginning in 2011, NAMB non-appointed missionary spouses were no longer included in the count. Also, this year most of the reduction was due to eliminating most MSC (self-funded) missionaries

++Beginning in 2015, NAMB missionary count includes missionaries, church planters, church planting team members, and student missionaries.

+++Beginning in 2019, NAMB's missionary count fluctuates because most are church planters who rotate out five years after their church launches.

GCR did not boost significantly the giving of Southern Baptists to their mission boards or increase the number of missionaries on the field for either board. The creation of the Great Commission Giving category created an uproar at the time, but there is no evidence that it stimulated fresh support (new money) for either CP giving or Great Commission Giving. Could all the effort given to magnify the importance of designated giving have been better spent in an effort to reinvigorate excitement for and commitment to the Cooperative Program and the annual mission offerings?

Most importantly, the number of missionaries deployed by both the International Mission Board and the North American Mission boards also significantly decreased by the end of the decade.

Southern Baptists will never know. Most agree CP is absolutely critical to the health of the shared ministries of the Southern Baptist Convention. Perhaps an opportunity to excite the rising generation about the genius of the Cooperative Program and its performance relative to the designated support model used by other American church families was missed in the shift from a single focus on CP to a divided focus on CP and Great Commission Giving.

GCR did not boost significantly the giving of Southern Baptists to their mission boards or increase the number of missionaries on the field for either board.

According to the *SBC Annual*, in 2007 SBC churches gave a record high $205,716,834 to the SBC portion of the Cooperative Program. Will they ever get back to that level of giving and more? Any increase in CP distribution to the mission boards or other SBC entities without an increase in the total amount of CP to be distributed is illusory growth obtained by making other budget categories smaller. During the decade following the approval of the GCR proposals, the SBC received a larger portion of the Cooperative Program pie, but the pie itself has not yet returned to the 2010 level of total CP income. Because the SBC received a larger slice from a clearly smaller pie, the SBC CP remains significantly below the 2007 record high of $205,716,834. The crucial fiscal challenge facing Southern Baptists is how to make the pie bigger, not how to make any particular slice of the pie bigger. This challenge is particularly true in light of the effect of inflation on actual buying power. None of these numbers factor in the growth of inflation. What is true for families is true for churches, mission boards, and missionaries. As inflation grows higher, the actual buying power of gifts given is reduced.

Any increase in CP distribution to the mission boards or other SBC entities without an increase in the total amount of CP to be distributed is illusory growth obtained by making other budget categories smaller.

SBC Giving Trends (2010-2021)

Year	Total Receipts by SBC Churches	Total Undesignated Gifts to SBC Churches	Total CP
2010	$10,680,023,357	$8,911,796,522	$500,410,514
2011	$11,805,027,705	$9,023,216,896	$487,884,065
2012	$11,521,418,784	$8,891,673,582	$481,409,006
2013	$11,209,655,950	$8,769,026,657	$482,279,059
2014	$11,154,665,938	$8,748,114,744	$478,700,850
2015	$11,545,861,631	$9,154,427,472	$474,272,984
2016	$11,461,572,538	$9,216,198,700	$475,212,293
2017	$11,728,420,088	$9,518,527,051	$462,662,332
2018	$11,811,093,609	$9,601,534,950	$463,076,368
2019	$11,640,670,559	$9,600,108,179	$462,299,010
2020	$11,526,598,340	$9,531,225,749	$455,553,027
2021	$11,830,303,965	$9,774,807,128	$457,928,996

Year	Total State CP	Total SBC CP	Total CP % of Undesignated Gifts
2010	$308,647,361	$191,763,153	5.62%
2011	$301,498,029	$186,386,036	5.41%
2012	$294,768,525	$186,640,481	5.41%
2013	$298,859,256	$183,419,803	5.50%
2014	$297,729,271	$180,971,579	5.47%
2015	$290,501,682	$183,771,302	5.18%
2016	$284,743,512	$190,468,781	5.16%

2017	$270,713,506	$191,948,826	4.86%
2018	$271,818,380	$191,257,988	4.82%
2019	$271,331,607	$190,967,403	4.82%
2020	$267,746,391	$187,806,636	4.78%
2021	$270,153,074	$187,775,922	4.68%

Chart prepared from Annual of the Southern Baptist Convention, 2010-2021 and 2022 SBC Book of Reports (Executive Committee Reports).

The SBC Executive Committee defines Great Commission Giving as the total amount of all money given to all Southern Baptist mission causes by SBC congregations. This total amount includes monies given to: Cooperative Program, Annie Armstrong and Lottie Moon offerings, PLUS monies given to associations, state conventions (such as a state mission offering), and any other Southern Baptist mission cause. With that many different income streams, Great Commission Giving is guaranteed to produce a large total of dollars. Key questions are: Will it stimulate greater giving to those income streams that are so crucial to SBC ministry? Will the large figure of total dollars provide useful insight that will increase understanding into what is happening in the world of Southern Baptist giving? The chart below shows the total amount included in the Great Commission Giving category for each year from its beginning in 2011 through the 2021 fiscal year.

Annual Great Commission Giving (2011-2021)

Year	Great Commission Giving
2011	$695,694,322
2012	$744,043,625
2013	$777,452,820
2014	$637,498,179
2015	$613,201,805
2016	$646,017,306
2017	$593,980,600
2018	$572,281,994
2019	$540,859,296
2020	$409,835,470
2021	$516,093,240

Chart prepared from Annual of the Southern Baptist Convention, 2010-2021 (EC Reports).

To summarize: The creation of the great Commission Giving category was one of the highest priorities for the GCR Task Force. It was to be the stimulus to create a fresh commitment to sacrificial giving to fund the Great Commission enterprise. Instead, Great Commission Giving became yet another illustration of the growing decline of the Southern Baptist Convention. This "kitchen sink" of a category that includes giving to all SBC mission causes produces a big number, but it does not reveal the health or lack of health for any particular catego-

The crucial fiscal challenge facing Southern Baptists is how to make the pie bigger, not how to make any particular slice of the pie bigger.

ry. Only one thing stands out: Southern Baptists are giving less to all mission causes than they did before the GCR proposals were adopted. In fact, they are giving less and have a smaller mission enterprise now than they did in 2010. Unless present trends are reversed, the future for Southern Baptists is likely to include serious financial challenges.

Component Four: Reaching North America

Component Four is the true heart of the Great Commission Resurgence proposals. Changes in the relationships between the North American Mission Board and the state Baptist conventions and the massive shift away from evangelism and to church planting have had a profound impact on SBC life, and not in a good way. The outcomes of NAMB's GCR-based strategy for the last decade appear to me to be a red flag warning to Southern Baptists.

We ask Southern Baptists to unleash the North American Mission Board for a new era of leadership and service to Southern Baptists, pushing back against the lostness of the United States and Canada.

The reinvention of the North American Mission Board that we envision will implement a missional strategy for planting churches in North America with a priority to reach metropolitan areas and underserved people groups.

It is our desire that at least 50% of the ministry efforts of our North American Mission Board be given to assist churches in planting healthy, multiplying, and faithful Baptist congregations in the United States and Canada.

We also call for NAMB to reclaim its mission of assisting churches to make disciples, working with Lifeway Christian Resources and other partners.

Similarly, we call for NAMB to be prioritized with the task of leadership development through the development of current pastoral leadership, with particular attention to contextual evangelism and church planting.

We call upon NAMB to penetrate lostness in partnership with state conventions located in the most unreached and underserved populations of North America.

We encourage NAMB to set a goal of phasing out all Cooperative Agreements within seven years and to establish a new pattern of strategic partnership with the state conventions that will penetrate lostness and ensure a greater responsiveness to the Southern Baptist Convention and greater effectiveness for NAMB in the appointment of missionary personnel and church planters (2010 SBC Annual, pp. 83-85).

Ten years after its adoption, the controversy over Great Commission Giving is fading into the background of the SBC, representing more of a lost opportunity to excite a rising generation about the Cooperative Program, than a major disruption of existing CP support. Data indicate CP giving was not re-energized, but the bottom did not drop out. Component Four, however, was in effect a makeover of the North American Mission Board approach to its mission in a way that brought into question a fundamental principle of Baptist polity. Also, as a result of these GCR recommendations new ministry assignments were added to NAMB and its historic focus on evangelism was downplayed even as SBC churches struggled to reach the lost in their communities. The abandonment of key aspects of its historic partnership with the state conventions was strongly encouraged. The results were far below expectations. The passing of a decade has revealed the lasting legacy of the Great Commission Resurgence emerged from the proposals in Component Four, the true heart of GCR. These were profound changes rather than strategic adjustments, and they have had a deep impact with troubling effects.

Proposals one, six, and seven of Component Four as previously listed are different ways to recommend a revolutionary change in the relationship between the North American Mission Board and the state Baptist conventions, by far the most profound change suggested in the GCR proposals. The first proposal in Component Four was for the SBC to

---

The passing of a decade has revealed the lasting legacy of the Great Commission Resurgence emerged from the proposals in Component Four, the true heart of GCR. These were profound changes rather than strategic adjustments, and they have had a deep impact with troubling effects.

"unleash" the North American Mission Board to enable it to better accomplish its mission. A crucial assumption underlies this part of the GCR proposal. Although not explained, the task force said, "The central concern of all was the priority of liberating NAMB to conduct and direct a strategy of reaching the United States and Canada with the Gospel and planting Gospel churches." (*2010 SBC Annual*, p. 83) Perhaps when documents of the task force are unsealed at the end of the fifteen-year lockdown, Southern Baptists will learn the source of this idea that NAMB was being kept on a leash. The task force asked Ed Stetzer, then a researcher at NAMB, to prepare a white paper (formal analysis) describing why NAMB was being hindered in its mission.

Proposals one, six, and seven of Component Four as listed above are different ways to recommend a revolutionary change in the relationship between the North American Mission Board and the state Baptist conventions, by far the most profound change suggested in the GCR proposals.

Stetzer on NAMB as "One Hindered Effort"

The title of Stetzer's paper was "One Hindered Effort." It was submitted to the Great Commission Task Force on October 4, 2009. After summarizing the history of the Home Mission Board/NAMB efforts to accomplish its assigned mission, he suggested several problems affected the NAMB of 2010. Among those problems were:

- Lack of a compelling organizational vision;
- Lack of accountability for results;
- Perception of irrelevance in the present and the future by many in the SBC;
- Emergence of successful churches creating and resourcing their own networks to teach, create resources, and do church planting and missions;
- Limitations of the Cooperative Program model;
- Internal leadership issues involving both competence and uncertainty over the role of Trustees at NAMB; and
- Autonomy of Southern Baptist churches, state conventions, and associations.

Stetzer felt strongly that NAMB had too many assigned areas of responsibility to be able to maintain a clear focus internally and externally on the mission of reaching North America. Apparently, more compelling than any of these issues to the Task Force was the attention given by Stetzer to a problem created by Baptist polity. The autonomy of

Southern Baptist churches, state conventions, and associations meant there was no clear, centralized control over who did what in order to reach North America for Christ. Churches, associations, state conventions, and NAMB were all working toward that end, but no one person, church, or entity was in charge of managing the whole domestic mission enterprise for Southern Baptists. Stetzer failed to note two things. First, given historic Southern Baptist polity, this was exactly what one would expect to be the case. Second, in spite of limitations growing out of this polity, Southern Baptists were able to work through the challenges and become the largest Protestant denomination in the United States.

Perhaps there was no central control over efforts to reach North America because the churches of the SBC did not need a controlling authority as much as they needed a resource and support center to facilitate their work of reaching North America for Christ.

One matter given little attention in Southern Baptist life is the fundamental difference between the work of the International Mission Board and the North American Mission Board. Given the vastly different assignments and contexts of the two mission boards, Southern Baptists should expect them to be very different in their approach to their missions. Southern Baptists took a long time to realize this and figure out the best and most effective way to utilize a mission board focused on helping churches reach this nation.

The first century of the newly created Southern Baptist Convention reflected a frustrating struggle as the churches of the Convention tried to figure out how all the churches could cooperate together to reach the nation without interfering with each other or violating the sacred Baptist principle of autonomy. According to Stetzer, lack of communication between the state conventions and the HMB, reduplication of efforts with the HMB doing the same things in the same places as state conventions and associations, thus wasting resources unnecessarily, and a lack of clarity on who was doing what were issues frequently raised in SBC life of that era. It was a very different challenge than that facing the International Mission Board and its mission of going into nations with little or no Gospel witness already in place. With thousands of churches across the country, hundreds of associations, and many state conventions already in place and firmly rooted, the early uncertainty surrounding the role of the Home Mission Board is unsurprising. It had partners in its mission whether it wanted them or not. While the IMB operated in a virtual vacuum with little or no Baptist presence on the scene, HMB/NAMB faced a field relatively crowded with Baptists. Given the different circumstances, one would expect the two boards to take different approaches.

As the second century of the SBC story unfolded, a strategy to manage this complex situation
emerged. Some began to ask: "What if a state convention and the Home Mission Board negotiated a
strategy for work in that state to create a clear agreement on who would do what and how each component of the strategy would be paid for?" Rather than
the HMB acting arbitrarily and independently on a
strategy for the nation developed in Atlanta, sup-
pose the Board and the state conventions planned a
strategy together for each region that incorporated
both national and regional priorities? The Baptist
General Convention of Texas and the HMB created the first such agreement, and it was embraced as
a model for the Board's relationships with all state
conventions and their churches. This was not one
identical agreement between HMB and all state conventions. It was a distinctive agreement between
HMB and each state convention, reflecting the particular circumstances and goals as perceived by each
convention and its churches, along with whatever
goals the HMB might have for that state. Thus, with
state by state strategic plans Southern Baptists created a regionally-based national strategy for reaching North America with clearly defined roles for the
state conventions, including their local churches and
associations, and the Home Mission Board.

In financial terms, the result was that Great
Commission strategies in every state convention

were funded by **both** the giving of churches in the state convention **and** the giving of all churches in the Southern Baptist Convention through CP and the Annie Armstrong Offering. Stronger conventions received a smaller percentage of budget support from CP. Newer conventions received a higher percentage of support for their budgets. This cooperative strategy requiring the agreement of both the state conventions and HMB/NAMB with all churches both contributing to and benefitting from the mutual support of CP meant all churches had "skin in the game" for building the Cooperative Program. There were clear reasons for the state conventions to promote and support the Cooperative Program and work with NAMB. It was a clever way to encourage a sense of SBC-wide partnership through CP. Most importantly, as Baptists began expanding outside the South, it provided early logistical support for new churches and emerging state conventions at their most vulnerable phase of development. The result was unprecedented success in the second half of the twentieth century.

Thus, with state by state strategic plans Southern Baptists created a regionally-based national strategy for reaching North America with clearly defined roles for the state conventions, including their local churches and associations, and the Home Mission Board.

The documents describing the relationships and roles of state conventions and HMB/NAMB were called Cooperative Agreements spelling out who did what and who paid for what. They were negotiated individually with each state convention on an annual basis with strategy coordinators from NAMB and the state convention staff, with each party knowing negotiations had to continue until they reached an agreement on all terms. One could well imagine negotiations were quite intense, and rarely were such agreements considered perfect by both parties. In spite of the obvious challenges, the process brought a level of communication and coordination between HMB/NAMB and the state conventions that had not been present for the first hundred years of the Convention's history. The inevitable tensions created by autonomous bodies working together never completely disappeared, but the path was cleared for the SBC to experience massive growth driven by this process of negotiated voluntary cooperation. Although messy at times, the Cooperative Agreements were undeniably fruitful. The Southern Baptist Convention became a truly national body with churches in all fifty states and associations and conventions in every region of the country. The Cooperative Program became woven into the fabric of Southern Baptists in every region of the country.

The SBC did periodic major reviews of the process through the years. Those reviews were noted and summarized by Stetzer. Typically, such reviews would make a tweak here and there but always conclude that the Cooperative Agreements may not have been perfect, but they needed to continue as the best solution to the complex problem of autonomous bodies cooperating to reaching the nation as a unified SBC. These Cooperative Agreements were the engine that drove the growth and expansion of Southern Baptists across the nation for decades. Awkward it might have been, but the cooperative process for evangelism, church planting, and ministry between the state conventions and HMB/NAMB got unprecedented results without a centralized control over the work of reaching North America with the Gospel. They also energized Cooperative Program promotion at the local and regional level. Stetzer summarized the situation with this comment:

> NAMB's structure and its relationship with the state conventions are still issues of discussion, although most now assume this structure as the standard. For most people in denominational life, it is their understanding that NAMB works THROUGH states rather than IN the states. This approach is both a help (providing NAMB with strong partnerships when it works well) and a hindrance (when no one has clear responsibility or accountability). (Stetzer, "One Hindered Effort" (p. 9).

Awkward it might have been, but the cooperative process for evangelism, church planting, and ministry between the state conventions and HMB/NAMB got unprecedented results without a centralized control over the work of reaching North America with the Gospel.

The Cooperative Agreements were a strategic partnership in every sense of the term. Both parties had a voice in determining how to proceed, but neither could do well without the engagement of the other. There were benefits for both when the strategy worked smoothly, and there were consequences for both when it did not. The bottom line: after struggling for a hundred years, the SBC finally had a regionally-based national strategy to reach the whole of North America with the Gospel, and it worked.

THE GREAT SHIFT

One member of the GCR Task Force is well known among his colleagues for saying never appoint a study committee until after you have determined what the outcome of the study will be. Indeed, by asking Stetzer to do a paper answering the question, "What has hindered NAMB from fulfilling its mission," the Task Force decided before commissioning Setzer's paper that they wanted revolutionary change at the North American Mission Board. Apparently, that revolutionary change was a shift away from a true partnership with state conventions and associations reflecting regional and local priorities in a shared strategy of evangelism and church planting. The GCR Task Force wanted a single corporate strategy with clear strategic control and direction from NAMB offices in Atlanta. Control was the operative word. In the words of the task force:

> We encourage NAMB to set a goal of phasing out all Cooperative Agreements within seven years, and establish a new pattern of strategic partnership with the state conventions that will penetrate lostness and *ensure greater responsiveness to the Southern Baptist Convention* [italics mine] and great effectiveness for NAMB in the appointment of missionary personnel and church planters (*2010 SBC Annual*, pp. 84-85).

The language above in italics is a remarkable shift away from historic Baptist polity. Control from an external source over any autonomous unit in Baptist life was a departure from normal in Southern Baptist life. For the GCR Task Force, central control by a national entity was preferred to the existing model of negotiated voluntary cooperation between autonomous Baptist bodies. The Task Force wanted the conventions created by the churches of a region to be more responsive to directive authority from the SBC through its entity, the North American Mission Board than to the churches those conventions served. This writer has not found a clearer step toward changing Baptist polity in the SBC story.

It is not likely that the GCR Task Force set out deliberately to change Baptist polity. It is more likely that they were conflating the work of the two mission boards into one operational philosophy in spite of the vast difference in their settings. The International Mission Board might appoint a missionary to plant a church in a South Asian city teeming with millions of people but having no Baptist witness. Its partners in the effort are Southern Baptists thousands of miles away who are completely unaffected by this action. When NAMB appoints a church planter to start a church in Atlanta, Seattle, Miami, the DFW metroplex, or Chicago, the situation is very different. These cities are also teeming with millions of people, but in addition they have an existing Baptist base already present. There are many churches already in place. There is an association formed by the existing churches. There is a state convention created by those existing churches. It is highly likely those associations and state conventions have a plan in mind for church planting in those cities. It is highly likely they have enlisted churches to help start new churches in that area. NAMB cannot approach its mission in the same way as the IMB. Whether or not it wants them, NAMB has partners who are affected by nearly everything it does to reach North America. Coordination and communication are far bigger issues for Southern Baptist success than control. If you damage Baptist work already in place when you start something new, you have not advanced the Gospel.

The Task Force expected some form of partnership to replace the existing state partnerships, but they wanted it to be a partnership with NAMB clearly in charge of reaching North America. The partnership would be more corporate in nature, with NAMB as the senior partner and the state conventions as junior partners, creating greater separation between state conventions and NAMB and between new church plants and the state conventions. Perhaps the classic maxim from the secular business world reflects what was in mind: "We operate by the Golden Rule. He who has the gold, rules." The money given to NAMB through CP and the Annie Armstrong Offering became the tool to implement the central control which replaced the strategic partnership model. When cooperation was not required, funding support became optional. NAMB could change at will any strategic priorities, job descriptions, or personnel that historically included some form of NAMB funding, without obligation to state conventions or associational processes and without consulting the churches in the region or the state conventions and associations created by those churches. The Task Force wanted revolutionary change, and this change was indeed revolutionary.

The termination of the Cooperative Agreements gave NAMB the potential power to create a financial crisis for state conventions and associations that differed with the corporate strategy coming out of Atlanta. Based on interviews with those who worked in the more vulnerable regions of the SBC, the non-South conventions and associations, NAMB used that power, and financial crises did emerge in several state conventions.

The GCR Task Force wanted a single corporate strategy with clear strategic control and direction from NAMB offices in Atlanta. Control was the operative word.

Much fanfare accompanied the task force recommendation that NAMB decentralize for a more regional approach to reach the nation. NAMB publicly embraced the idea and announced a reorganization with five regional Vice Presidents who would live and work with the conventions, associations, and churches of their assigned region. That ideal was started but never fully realized. The positions began to be discontinued before all five were filled, and today there are no regional VPs listed in the corporate directory of NAMB found in the *SBC Annual*. Even with the regional VP approach, those in that position would still have been employees of NAMB, not the churches in the region. Strategy and central control moved relentlessly toward Atlanta.

The Task Force wanted the conventions created by the churches of a region to be more responsive to directive authority from the SBC through its entity, the North American Mission Board than to the churches those conventions served. This writer has not found a clearer step toward changing Baptist polity in the SBC story.

The reality is that for decades the Cooperative Agreements had given Southern Baptists a decentralized, regional approach to reach the nation. HMB/NAMB was at the center of that strategy, providing resources, support, and connections with other Southern Baptists, but not at the top exercising control and direction. Being at the center rather than the top does make a difference. A decade down the road, it now appears the Task Force recommendations were actually a rejection of decentralization in favor of giving the North American Mission Board the means to control efforts to reach the nation from Atlanta, particularly those efforts outside the South. Any concerns over weakening at best or losing completely at worst the strategic partnerships that drove the growth of the SBC for decades were judged worth sacrificing in order to establish the centralized control of NAMB over much of the effort to reach North America.

There is nothing wrong with attempting change, provided of course, that the change introduced produces positive fruit. Radical change at NAMB did grow out of these proposals, but the ten years following those changes produced an epic evangelism crisis and the worst decade of church statistics in SBC history. The reader will see that data indicates the

> *Whether or not it wants them, NAMB has partners who are affected by nearly everything it does to reach North America.*

"unleashed" NAMB became the less fruitful NAMB. The lack of communication, reduplication of efforts and confusion over who is doing what that characterized the era before the Cooperative Agreements soon returned to the SBC.

THE EVANGELISM OMISSION

Proposals two and three of Component Four incorporated a different kind of shift. The focus of the Home Mission Board in its earliest years was church planting (then called church extension) and what today's Baptists would call compassion (social) ministries. Those two priorities became three in 1906, when SBC messengers requested the Home Mission Board create a Department of Evangelism to assist SBC churches in reaching their communities for Christ. Immediately, evangelism was added as an HMB priority and became one of the threefold emphases of the Board (See *Fuel the Fire* by Charles Kelley). For decades every HMB/NAMB President reporting to the Convention would typically begin his report by telling messengers of the entity's primary focus on three ministries: evangelism, church planting, and ministry to human needs. The task force, however, recommended that NAMB reinvent itself by focusing "at least 50% of the ministry efforts" on church plant-

The Task Force wanted revolutionary change, and this change was indeed revolutionary.

ing (*2010 SBC Annual*, p. 84). The term "contextual evangelism" was used once in passing without any explanation or elaboration. The task force may have assumed direct evangelism would remain a priority for NAMB, but they did not make that assumption clear in any of the seven GCR components proposed for Convention action. The historic responsibility of NAMB to emphasize and support evangelism in Southern Baptist life was ignored.

The significance of the evangelism omission became apparent when NAMB's new leadership took control after the approval of the GCR proposals. On the basis of the GCR recommendations, NAMB made a hard turn away from promoting and funding evangelism with major reductions in staff, programs, resources and promotional activity, including funding for evangelism in state conventions. Evangelism was dropped from its traditional place as one of the three primary ministries of the North American Mission Board. After the GCR approval, Southern Baptists were repeatedly told at SBC meetings and on the NAMB website that the primary focus of NAMB was on the Send Network (church planting) and Send Relief (compassion ministry). In the words of the NAMB president to the 2019 SBC: "We serve pastors and churches in two primary ways: Send Relief, our compassion ministry, and Send Network, our church planting network" (*2019 SBC Annual*, p. 204).

The reality is that for decades the Cooperative Agreements had given Southern Baptists a decentralized, regional approach to reach the nation. HMB/NAMB was at the center of that strategy, providing resources, support, and connections with other Southern Baptists, but not at the top exercising control and direction.

Attention to evangelism was noticeably absent. This was made clear yet again in the NAMB report to the 2021 SBC meeting. Messengers were told, "Our goal is to have highly qualified missionaries who are keenly focused on our primary ministry areas of church planting and compassion ministry" (*2021 SBC Annual*, p. 243). A decade after GCR and in the midst of the greatest evangelism crisis in the history of the SBC, NAMB wanted missionaries who were "keenly focused" on church planting and compassion ministry. But not evangelism.

After more than 100 years as a primary focus point for the Home Mission Board and its successor the North American Mission Board, evangelism was relegated to the back bench. NAMB did not completely eliminate evangelism, but in the years following the GCR adoption, its role, funding, and promotional priority diminished dramatically. The Board is no longer capable of putting together a strategic initiative on the scale of *God's Plan for Sharing*, so awkwardly shelved after GCR. It would take years to rebuild the capacity for what Southern Baptists could once do.

The reader will see that data indicates the "unleashed" NAMB became the less fruitful NAMB.

Perhaps the new NAMB leadership assumed evangelism would happen without giving it much attention. If so, they took the opposite approach to church planting. A comprehensive strategic plan supported by massive increases in budget support was developed, with constant promotional activity. A complex process for enlisting churches in church planting, identifying potential church planters, and evaluating, training, and deploying candidates selected for the church planter "pipeline" and church planter internships and residencies were put in place. An unprecedented nurture and encouragement process for church planters was established, along with the purchase of single-family homes for church planters as well as properties for church facilities. No comparable national strategic plan to encourage evangelism in SBC churches exists, in spite of the Board's SBC ministry assignment to produce such a plan. No report on progress towards the development of such a plan has ever been made to the Convention.

The reinvention called for by the GCR Task Force happened. NAMB is going about its mission in a completely different way. The crucial question is: How is this new approach working in terms of outcomes? Did church planting prosper after the change? Did the nearly exclusive focus on church planting and compassion (social) ministry ignite fresh passion for the Great Commission? In other words: Was the evangelistic fruitfulness of SBC churches affected by these changes?

New Assignments

The fourth proposal included in Component Four is both ironic and confusing. It is ironic in that it completely ignores a recommendation made in Stetzer's white paper. Stetzer suggested that NAMB had little chance of a clear focus on the task of reaching North America with the Gospel because its ministry assignment from the SBC included far too many issues for the Board to address effectively. He strongly recommended that NAMB's mission statement be simplified. Instead, the fourth proposal recommended adding something new to NAMB's assignment. In the words of the task force:

> We also call for NAMB to reclaim its mission of assisting churches to make disciples, working with Lifeway Christian Resources and other partners (2010 SBC Annual, p. 84).

The mystery of this recommendation is that there was no past discipleship assignment to reclaim. Discipleship had always been the central task of the Sunday School Board and its successor Lifeway. This is probably why the task force suggested NAMB work on this assignment with "Lifeway Christian Resources and other partners." If this recommendation would take NAMB out of its lane in SBC life, there had to be some connection with those who had the historic responsibility. Discipleship was never assigned to the Home Mission Board. The North American Mission Board was formed in 1995-96 and launched in 1997 as part of a massive SBC reorganization effort called the Covenant for a New

Century. The Home Mission Board, the Radio and Television Commission, and the Brotherhood Commission were combined to create the North American Mission Board. The words "make disciples" or "discipleship" were not used at any point in the ministry assignment for the newly formed NAMB recommended to and approved by the SBC (1995 SBC Annual, p. 166-7).

Through the years, periodic tension flared between the Sunday School Board/Lifeway and the Home Mission Board/NAMB, but the issue was not discipleship. The tensions between the Boards were over the responsibility for church growth. The Convention eventually got involved and made clear the responsibility of the Sunday School Board for church growth and the Home Mission Board for evangelism. Discipleship, as it pertains to helping believers grow in their faith and spiritual maturity, was never a focal point for either the former Home Mission Board or

On the basis of the GCR recommendations, NAMB made a hard turn away from promoting and funding evangelism with major reductions in staff, programs, resources and promotional activity, including funding for evangelism in state conventions. Evangelism was dropped from its traditional place as one of the three primary ministries of the North American Mission Board.

the newly created North American Mission Board that succeeded it. The only NAMB discussions related to discipleship were about the specific issue of immediate follow-up materials for new Christians, a natural question flowing from strategic thinking about evangelism.

The pre-GCR NAMB was highly focused on evangelism. Perhaps that focus was why NAMB leaders in the past did not pursue the task of discipleship even though they were concerned about helping new believers get started following Jesus. The resulting discussion between NAMB and Sunday School Board/Lifeway on who should handle follow-up for new believers was resolved amicably. All agreed the Sunday School Board/Lifeway was on point to address immediate follow-up as well as the long-term issue of discipleship for all Southern Baptists. The *Survival Kit for New Christians* was written with immediate follow-up in mind by Ralph Neighbor Jr, an evangelism employee for the Home Mission Board. By mutual agreement it was published and distributed by Lifeway and widely promoted by the Home Mission Board in their emphasis on follow up for those who came to Christ. The resource was very popular, becoming the best-selling tool on follow-up after conversion that Southern Baptists ever produced. Again, attention was on the need to follow up with new converts as opposed to helping churches address the issue of ongoing discipleship. Perhaps when the documents of the task force are unsealed, some insight on why this confusing recommendation was made will be revealed. The task force could have addressed Lifeway with recommendations pertaining to its historic assignment of discipleship, but chose not to do so.

Previous research did lead this writer to conclude that discipleship is a major issue that deeply affects evangelism. Virtually every strategy for evangelism ever conceived and implemented in the history of the church begins with the assumption that the life of a Christian is distinctively different than that of an unbeliever. A distinctive life is the fruit of discipleship, but the responsibility for that kind of discipleship has never been bundled with the responsibility for evangelism and included for NAMB in the list of its responsibilities as assigned by Southern Baptists. This is due in large part to the obvious connection between Bible study and discipleship, making the Sunday School Board/Lifeway the natural home for this assignment. The question is not on the importance of discipleship, but rather on what entity is best suited to promote it in Southern Baptist life and assist local churches in addressing the issue. The decision of the task force to ignore the historic role of Lifeway and recommend that NAMB address discipleship was a new, unexpected assignment going against the grain of long SBC tradition and practice.

The fifth proposal in Component Four called for NAMB to make the task of leadership development with current pastoral leadership a high priority:

> *Similarly, we call for NAMB to be prioritized with the task of leadership development through the development of current pastoral leadership, with particular attention to contextual evangelism and church planting. NAMB must become a central engine for building missional momentum among Southern Baptist pastors* (2010 SBC Annual, p. 84).

This was a request to add a second new area to the SBC ministry assignment for the North American Mission Board. Although including this as a specific ministry assignment was new, NAMB had been somewhat engaged in the work of leadership development for several years.

Leadership was a passionate concern for Dr. Bob Reccord, the founding president of NAMB. There is no indication that Reccord ever sought to adjust the SBC ministry assignment for NAMB to include leadership development, but soon after he began his tenure, he implemented leadership training and development as a major emphasis. His reports to the SBC typically began with the traditional threefold emphasis on evangelism, church planting, and ministry to needs, As he would describe what the Board had done in response to its ministry assignments each year, the language of leadership development always found a place in regard to one or more of those three priority assignments. Most often the places where leadership was emphasized were in regard to the appointment of missionaries and NAMB's work with associations. Stetzer noted in his white paper that Reccord's vision for NAMB seemed to be at odds with that of his Trustees. He spent ever larger amounts of money on leadership programs, resources, and events, not all of which were successful. Stetzer did not go into much detail, but internal conflict within the NAMB family in those days was a reality. Many thought the large emphasis on leadership was a significant factor in that conflict.

The Task Force recommended a leadership development focus that gave particular attention to contextual evangelism and church planting. Contextual evangelism is not a common term among Southern Baptists. It suggests approaching the sharing of the gospel in light of the cultural distinctives of any particular setting. It is one of the only uses of the word "evangelism" in the task force recommendations and was not given any explanations or applications. Church planting is also not given further explanation or application in the context of leadership development, other than to speak of giving attention to current pastors as opposed to future or potential pastors. The only application given was for NAMB to use these emphases to build "mission-al momentum" among Southern Baptist pastors.

The Task Force did not explain why they recom-mended leadership development be made a clear pri-ority for NAMB. Perhaps past conflict over efforts to magnify leadership for whatever reason encouraged them to make a clear statement. Perhaps they felt a Great Commission Resurgence could not happen if NAMB was not driving the issue of leadership devel-opment in the SBC. We do not know. Adding the two new assignments of making disciples and leadership development to NAMB's list of responsibilities does make the absence of an emphasis on the historic pri-ority of evangelism even more mystifying.

Non-South Convention Partnerships

The sixth and final proposal included in Component Four acknowledged the need for NAMB to work in partnership with state conventions even though the historic structure of Cooperative Agreements was completely rejected. NAMB was particularly asked to work closely with state conventions outside the Baptist stronghold of the South.

> *We call upon NAMB to penetrate lostness in part-nership with state conventions located in the most*

unreached and underserved populations of North
America (2010 SBC Annual, p. 84).

Whatever form a partnership with state conventions might take, the task force was clearly concerned
that careful attention be given to working closely
with the state conventions facing the largest challenges. This was not a new concern. As noted earlier, the
white paper by Ed Stetzer documented that the place
of NAMB in the SBC has been uneasy from the creation of the Board for Domestic Missions established
at the birth of the SBC in 1845. The awkwardness
comes from the presence of churches, associations
and state conventions already in existence.

The most obvious problem facing HMB/NAMB
and the state conventions is a reduplication of efforts with different SBC units attempting to accomplish the same mission in the same places at the same
time. This historic tension bubbled up in Baptist life
from time to time with various task forces or committees assigned to study the situation. The typical
conclusions of such studies were that the tensions
were inevitable, but the Cooperative Agreements
strategy should continue any way. Invariably such
task forces or committees would also express a desire for the HMB/NAMB to spend and work less in
places where Baptists had a strong presence in order to spend more and do more where the Baptist
presence was smaller and the work more difficult.

NAMB was expected to bring help to state conventions and fellowships in areas where Baptists were struggling to begin or strengthen their presence.

Yet again and again another reality surfaced. The work of HMB/NAMB had to include work in all state conventions including the stronger conventions in the South. There is a steadily growing population of lost people in the South, being fed by an increasing flow of people from the Northeast and the West Coast. The rust belt is losing people to the attractions of the sun belt. Millions of lost people in the South need to hear the Gospel. Thousands of new churches are needed in the South, and compassion ministry needs in the South are impossible to ignore. The tension of prioritizing needs when needs are everywhere is inevitable. It is a discussion that is unlikely to ever be settled once and for all. The typical conclusion of all the studies about the role of HMB/NAMB through the years can be summarized in this simple statement: Spend and work as much as you must in all state conventions, but diligently pursue doing more in places with a smaller Baptist presence.

The task force made their intent regarding non-South state conventions very clear. They strongly recommended the North American Mission Board work actively with the state conventions with a smaller Baptist presence. It is important to note that they did not suggest merely working in the non-

South states. They suggested NAMB work in and through the state conventions in the areas of the country with largely unchurched populations (*2010 SBC Annual*, p. 84). Unlike many of the other recommendations for NAMB, this recommendation appears to have been largely ignored.

WHAT HAPPENED?

The most profound impact of the Great Commission Resurgence actions came from the cluster of proposals focused on remaking the North American Mission Board. Those proposals included:

- Eliminating Cooperative Agreements between NAMB and the state conventions
- Modifying historic Baptist polity concerning complete autonomy
- Using at least 50% of NAMB budget for Church Planting, in a shift away from evangelism
- Adding two new ministry assignments (discipleship and leadership development)

The Trustees of NAMB were in the process of putting together a new executive team when the GCR recommendations were made. Once in place the new leadership team made it very clear that they were going to focus on implanting the recommendations from the task force, and they have to some extent. Most recommendations were accepted. However, some were ignored.

Now that a decade has passed, this researcher is unaware of any other SBC-approved actions that have had such profound negative effects on the ministry outcomes of SBC churches. One does not have to compare this decade with any other decade in SBC history to come to this conclusion. The comparison of the statistical snapshot of the SBC as it was in 2010 when the GCR proposals were approved with the statistical snapshot of the SBC as it is after ten years of implementation is a breathtaking downward change. Far from igniting a fresh passion for the Great Commission, the GCR proposals as implemented by the North American Mission Board seemed to push SBC churches toward a growing apathy toward reaching the lost people in their communities. Very unexpected was the increasing decline in church planting that followed the implementation of the new church planting strategy from NAMB, in spite of the huge budget increase that accompa-

Now that a decade has passed, this researcher is unaware of any other SBC-approved actions that have had such profound negative effects on the ministry outcomes of SBC churches.

nied the new strategy. This is not a criticism of the people involved in GCR or NAMB. It is an observation of the outcomes following a decade of implementation or lack thereof of GCR proposals. No other decade in SBC history has seen such a broad statistical decline in the standard measures applied to SBC churches, including the decade of the Great Depression and the decade of the tumultuous sixties.

Proposals One, Six, and Seven included in Component Four recommended a dramatic change in the relationship between the North American Mission Board and the state conventions by eliminating the Cooperative Agreements that had defined how these autonomous units worked together for decades. NAMB leadership fully embraced this recommendation. According to long-time Baptist journalist Joe Westbury, some $51 million in annual funding was removed from state conventions and associations (Joe Westbury, "State Conventions beyond the South Question SBC North American mission Board's Spending and Accountability for Church Planting, www.baptistnews.com February 18, 2021). The *Annual of the Southern*

> *No other decade in SBC history has seen such a broad statistical decline in the standard measures applied to SBC churches, including the decade of the Great Depression and the decade of the tumultuous sixties.*

Baptist Convention in the years following the GCR implementation confirms millions upon millions of dollars were taken away from the state conventions and associations who had been NAMB partners for decades. For smaller state conventions NAMB arbitrarily changed job descriptions for positions they had been supporting or eliminated them entirely. People who were hired as Directors of Missions were declared to be church planting catalysts or out of a job. In a letter to the editor of the New Mexico Baptist paper, published in November 2020, a former NAMB team leader wrote: "In March 2011, 120 missionaries serving in western states were told they were no longer needed." He suggested that "Ezell's agenda was to remove all the funding from western state conventions."

In the case of larger, stronger state conventions, different tactics were used to accomplish the same objective of withdrawing from historic partnerships. A NAMB insider who wishes to be anonymous provided an example of the approach. A large state convention was experiencing some fiscal challenges during a national economic downturn. The Cooperative Agreement with that state called for them to spend an allocation from NAMB for a specific Great Commission strategy. NAMB offered to release them from the Cooperative Agreement obligation and allow them to use the money any way they chose. In exchange for that flexibility of use, going forward NAMB would give that state convention a lesser amount of money, but let them use that money in any way they desired. The state executive accepted the deal, and the Cooperative Agreement was considered gone forever, as was the larger amount of money NAMB had been investing in shared Great Commission strategies. In this and similar strategies tailored to the circumstances of other state conventions, money was the tool used to gain centralized control over strategies created and driven by the Atlanta office. By allowing a more flexible use of some funds, NAMB began insisting on a more rigid use of other funds and control for Atlanta-based programs.

According to a report published in the *Christian Examiner* on May 4, 2016, NAMB added a twist to funds shared with at least some state conventions. When receiving funds from NAMB, at least some state executives are required to sign Non-Disclosure agreements that forbid them from discussing the money given or making critical comments about NAMB. Public comments about their dealings with the Board can result in the loss of funds for the state convention, and some say perhaps even the loss of employment. Many Southern Baptists have expressed concerns about the use of Non-Disclosure Agreements in cases of sexual abuse. One wonders how they would feel about Non-Disclosure Agreements related to Great Commission ministry funding. This does not appear to be a building block for healthy Convention relationships.

Proposal six of Component Four was closely related to one and seven, but it had a much more specific focus. Proposal six clearly recommended that NAMB work in partnership with state conventions located in the most unreached and underserved regions of North America. The West, the Northeast, and the Upper Midwest were widely regarded by Southern Baptists as much more unreached than the South. Through the years those regions were often called pioneer areas in SBC discussions. Only after the Cooperative Agreements had been created and implemented did Baptist work began to expand significantly in these areas. All understood that reaching these areas with the Gospel and planting churches in these areas were the most urgent Great Commission challenge facing the SBC. The North American Mission Board largely ignored this GCR recommendation. Having eliminated the Cooperative Agreements, *NAMB chose to do much more than simply not increase its support for non-South conventions. It actually pulled funding for evangelism and church planting out of several of these convention budgets, creating a fiscal crisis for the Great Commission work in the most unreached parts of North America.* NAMB insisted it was working in these regions, but it was not working through or in conjunction with the state conventions as the GCR Task Force had requested. Whether it was intended or not, GCR released a floodtide of communication breakdowns, reduplication of efforts, and great fiscal challenges for Baptist work outside of the South where the Great Commission needs were the greatest. In effect, NAMB began cutting state conventions it could not control out of the loop of its strategies.

This research project began with a series of blogs to document the growing problem of decline in the SBC. As the blogs were published, this writer started getting unsolicited contacts from various staff members working in different non-South state conventions. They always requested anonymity because, to use a phrase heard over and over again, "NAMB uses money like a weapon." A common theme in these conversations was the devastating effects of GCR on Baptist work in the most unreached parts of the country as a result of NAMB's new strategies.

Having eliminated the Cooperative Agreements, NAMB chose to do much more than simply not increase its support for non-South conventions. It actually pulled funding for evangelism and church planting out of several of these convention budgets, creating a fiscal crisis for the Great Commission work in the most unreached parts of North America.

Thus, it was not much of a surprise to this writer when six state convention executives in Western states came together to write a letter to NAMB Trustees and the SBC Executive Committee complaining that NAMB had abandoned the "true collaborative partnership" of former days, becoming far more centralized and unilateral in their approach. As a result, NAMB offered little value to these non-South state conventions and had become more of a competitor than a partner (See Appendix I). The letter further noted that NAMB was giving block grants of $300,000 to the larger, stronger Southern Conventions, while none of the non-South conventions were scheduled to receive anything like that amount in the coming year's NAMB budget. Far from the announced intention of GCR recommendations for NAMB to spend less in the stronger state conventions of the South in order to spend more in the much more challenged non-South conventions, the opposite was happening. NAMB did spend less in the South Conventions, but it also deeply reduced its spending in non-South conventions as well. Apparently the post-GCR NAMB wanted to disengage as much as possible from state convention partnerships in order to work independently and control completely Great Commission strategy for North America. As a consequence, the letter from state convention executives noted that several state convention boards were considering keeping more CP in the states and designating which SBC causes their CP gifts would support. NAMB's approach to the implementation of GCR recommendations was beginning to unravel the fabric of the Cooperative Program, a big part of the glue holding the SBC family together.

This letter was a bombshell unlike any other in SBC history. During the Conservative Resurgence, moderate leadership in the Baptist General Convention of Texas attempted to defund the six seminaries from Texas Cooperative Program gifts, but the churches of Texas forced them to back down from a total withdrawal of Texas CP support. This was different. The state executives of multiple conventions were questioning the value of continuing in the Cooperative Program because of the way their state conventions were being treated by the North American Mission Board. Prior to the NAMB implementation of the GCR recommendations, it was unthinkable that the Great Commission could create more turmoil and controversy than the theological battles of the Conservative Resurgence. The Cooperative Program was built on the shoulders of the state conventions. By design, all CP funds were collected from the churches by the state conventions. The state conventions would then forward to

> *NAMB's approach to the implementation of GCR recommendations was beginning to unravel the fabric of the Cooperative Program, a big part of the glue holding the SBC family together.*

the Southern Baptist Convention the amount of CP collected as determined by the churches of that convention. The state conventions had always played a critical role in the promotion of and the collection of all monies flowing into the Cooperative Program.

The GCR task force noted that this model which was built upon the state conventions is how CP was designed to work from the beginning (*2010 SBC Annual*, p. 86). The six state executives who drafted this letter were joined by nine other state executives shortly after the original letter was released. ***The decision of NAMB leadership to turn away from its historic support of multiple non-South state conventions in the most unreached regions of the nation, as a strategic decision, not an economic necessity, ranks as one of the more shocking decisions by an SBC entity in Convention history.*** Of even greater concern was that as the decade unfolded, NAMB appeared to have little interest in healthy, productive relationships with the many state conventions. Some in the non-South Conventions felt NAMB wanted to eliminate them altogether. After a decade, this perception was making support for the Cooperative Program weaker, not stronger.

According to a report in the *Louisiana Baptist Message* (September 24, 2020), the NAMB Trustee officers responded to the letter from the state conventions with complete indifference to their concerns. The officers insisted:

You have correctly identified that we are more focused (centralized) and directive in our strategies, personnel and funding. We're not sure you could make a more complimentary accusation of us (*LA Baptist Message*, September 24, 2020, p. 7).

More than a third of SBC state conventions had deep concerns over the actions of the North American Mission Board, and those concerns were deemed irrelevant to the staff and Trustees of NAMB. They considered the concerns of the state conventions to be a compliment. Such a response from one of the largest and most strategic entities of the Southern Baptist Convention to the concerns of Southern Baptist leaders serving in what all would agree are some of the most difficult settings for ministry faced by the Convention was inappropriate on an epic scale.

Clearly the Great Commission Resurgence did not result in getting more resources for evangelism and church planting to state conventions in the most unchurched, unreached areas of the nation. Quite the opposite. Non-South conventions like California and the Northwest were being systematically defunded. On October 2, 2020 *Baptist Press* reported on a somber consequence of NAMB's dismissive response to these state conventions. Tuesday, September 29, 2020 the Alaska Baptist Convention voted to retain in Alaska the percentage of CP funds intended for NAMB and designate them for a state mission fund "until such time as there is a collaborative, co-operative and mutually-agreed upon strategy with the North American Mission Board, as determined by our executive director and the executive board of the Alaska Baptist Resource Network."

In his article for *Baptist News Global*, Joe West-bury did an analysis of how NAMB changes in response to the GCR proposals specifically affected non-South state conventions. He discovered the consequences in many cases were severe. In addition to the massive funding hit, without the Cooperative Agreements in place, NAMB also began doing church planting in various state conventions without coordinating with or informing the state conventions where churches were started. This means that new churches being started by NAMB in areas with few Baptist churches were not being connected to the support network of state conventions and associations in their areas. This could have profound implications for the whole premise of the Southern Baptist Convention. The Convention came into being as a family of autonomous churches voluntarily cooperating with one another to reach the nation and the world with the Gospel, and together educating the ministers to serve that network of churches. Where will NAMB's new path take the SBC in the future when churches are started with CP money but not intentionally linked with existing SBC churches and ministries? Could NAMB be building a network of churches that would become a competitor to the SBC's traditional network of churches reflecting traditional Baptist polity?

As various members of state convention staffs told me directly, they had no idea when, where, or who was doing church planting in their states. The lack of communication and reduplication of efforts the Cooperative Agreements were created to prevent burst into full flower after the agreements were ended. Of even greater consequence, the GCR recommendations resulted in multiple state conventions beginning to rethink their participation in the Cooperative Program with the Southern Baptist Convention. Momentum to fulfill the Great Commission was not coming together.

Where will NAMB's new path take the SBC in the future when churches are started with CP money but not intentionally linked with existing SBC churches and ministries? Could NAMB be building a network of churches that would become a competitor to the SBC's traditional network of churches reflecting traditional Baptist polity?

In their letter to NAMB, the state executives asked the SBC Executive Committee to get involved as a mediator in this dispute. EC President Ronnie Floyd met separately with both parties to hear grievances and perspectives. Eventually he prepared a white paper entitled *Cooperation Is the Way Forward*, addressing the concerns of both parties and calling upon them to work out their differences for the sake of the Cooperative Program (See Appendix 1 for all three documents). Following the dialogues and the Floyd letter, Dr. Ezell did begin to meet with some of the state conventions and negotiate some increase in funding for specific projects if they would embrace the NAMB process of church planting. Significant tensions remain, but some progress in repairing the damage has been made. At their Fall 2022 state convention, Alaska Baptists acknowledged progress being made and renewed their commitment to CP and the Annie Armstrong Offering.

Proposals Two and Three of Component Four called upon NAMB to make church planting its major priority and devote at least fifty percent of its operating budget to church planting. NAMB enthusiastically complied with this proposal and now spends about $70 million a year on church planting, which is more than half of its operating budget. Since evangelism was barely mentioned in the GCR proposals to the Convention, NAMB made dramatic reductions in personnel, programs, resources, and promotion for evangelism. *God's Plan for Sharing*, the massive national evangelism strategic plan involving all the state conventions that began to unfold as the GCR proposals were approved, was quickly put on the back burner and stripped of its support team. Clearly, NAMB went all in on the GCR recommendation to make church planting its priority focus. What happened as a result was not what was expected.

In 2013, NAMB president Kevin Ezell told the Convention the SBC needed to start 1,500 new churches a year to keep pace with population growth and church closures (*2013 SBC Annual,* p. 177). In 2019, without explaining the change, he downsized the target to 1,200 new church starts a year (*2019 SBC Annual,* p. 205). By 2021, NAMB agreed with the SBC Executive Committee on an even further downsized goal of 600 new church plants a year until 2025 (*SBC Life Journal, Summer 2021,* p. 20). Apparently Southern Baptists are in danger of losing ground to the rising tide of lostness in the nation. With the post-GCR strategy for church planting in place for the last decade, the data on page 177ff indicate the Convention is becoming less likely to grow enough to offset its annual losses and the annual population gain.

One issue of growing concern is the continuing decline in the number of church planters available to start new churches. In 2010, NAMB reported 2,637 appointed/approved church planting missionaries. By 2011, the number dropped to 1,429. That was the last year NAMB announced the number of church planting missionaries in the SBC Annual. After multiple inquiries, NAMB, including the executive staff and its Trustee Chair, refused to release the number of appointed/approved church planting missionaries for any year since 2011, up to and including 2021, the last year for which official numbers should be available. No explanation for this refusal was given. It is extremely rare for an SBC entity to refuse to report good news in a basic category of its work. It is even more rare for any mission organization to not want its donors to know how many missionaries are working on its core mission. This lack of transparency about such basic information is unsettling and does not bode well for NAMB's progress. Eventually, after a very careful search of the NAMB website, this researcher was able to determine that NAMB had 1,316 church planters under appointment in 2021, a number NAMB officials refused to confirm or deny. This is half the number of church planting missionaries under appointment by NAMB in 2010 and 113 fewer than 2011 in spite of a massive increase in budget. Apparently, church planters who rotate out of the NAMB system are not being replaced on the same scale. NAMB has acknowledged to Southern Baptists that it does

After multiple inquiries, NAMB, including the executive staff and its Trustee Chair, refused to release the number of appointed/approved church planting missionaries for any year since 2011, up to and including 2021, the last year for which official numbers should be available.

not have the number of church planters it wants, attributing this to their high standards for church planters. If there are not enough church planters to implement its strategy, perhaps some strategic adjustments need to be made.

What follows is a series of charts with data taken from the official numbers published each year in the *Annual of the Southern Baptist Convention.* These charts are snapshots of SBC statistics, indicating the impact on SBC churches of NAMB's approach to implementing the GCR Proposals. At least a decade of statistics is included in each chart, providing a timeline to see developing trends. There has never been a decadal report weaker than the post-GCR decade in SBC history, including during the Great Depression.

The SBC After GCR (2010-2021)

Year	Total Churches	Church Plants	Total Members	Total Baptisms
2010	45,727	769	16,136,044	331,008
2011	45,764	1,003	15,978,112	333,341
2012	46,034	927	15,872,404	314,956
2013	46,125	936	15,735,640	310,368
2014	46,499	985	15,499,173	305,301
2015	46,793	926	15,294,764	295,262

2016	47,272	732	15,216,978	280,773
2017	47,544	691	15,005,638	254,122
2018	47,456	624	14,813,234	246,442
2019	47,530	552	14,525,579	235,748
2020	47,592	588	14,089,947	123,160
2021	47,614	600	13,680,493	154,701

Year	Baptisms Per Church	Worship Attendance	SBC Share of CP	SBC CP
2010	7.2	6,195,449	38.32%	$191,763,153
2011	7.2	6,155,116	38.20%	$186,386,036
2012	6.8	5,966,735	38.77%	$186,640,481
2013	6.7	5,834.707	38.03%	$183,419,803
2014	6.5	5,674,469	37.80%	$180,971,579
2015	6.3	5,577,088	38.75%	$183,771,302
2016	5.9	5,200,716	40.08%	$190,468,781
2017	5.3	5,320,488	41.49%	$191,948,826
2018	5.1	5,297,788	41.30%	$191,257,988
2019	4.9	5,250,230	41.31%	$196,731,703
2020	2.5	4,439,797	41.23%	$187,806,636
2021	3.2	3,607,530	41.01%	$187,775,922

Table created by Dr. Chuck Kelley, New Orleans, Baptist Theological Seminary, from data in the Annuals of the SBC (2010-2022)

Non-CP Churches in the SBC (2010-2021)

Year	Total SBC Churches	Non-CP SBC Churches	% of Non-CP SBC Churches
2010	46,640	13,897	29.79%
2011	46,410	16,134	34.76%
2012	46,713	16,493	35.30%
2013	46,877	16,692	36.60%
2014	48,147	18,675	38.78%
2015	47,746	18,220	38.16%
2016	48,265	18,151	37.60%
2017	48,585	18,931	38.96%
2018	48,494	18,996	39.17%
2019	48,709	19,645	40.33%
2020			
2021			

Data from SBC Life Journal, Summer 2021 and Annuals of the Southern Baptist Convention

Church Planting Before GCR (2000-2010)

Year	Church Planting Budget	Church Planting Missionaries	New Church Plants
2000	$20,795,536	2,266	1,681*
2001	$21,260,083	2,262	1,415*
2002	$19,670,397	2,331	1,606*
2003	$19,489,287	2,273	1,436*

2004	$20,215,355	2,196	1,781*
2005	$17,478,713	2,023	1,725*
2006	$20,637,289	2,003	1,458*
2007	$23,937,093	2,228	1,455*
2008	$21,681,540	2,741	1,397*
2009	$21,409,697	2,734	1,256*
2010	$20,873,256	2,637	769

Source: Annuals of the Southern Baptist Convention
*Includes church plants and newly affiliated churches

Total Church Planting Budget 2000-2010: $227,448,246
Net Increase in SBC Churches 2000-2010: 4,139

Church Planting After GCR (2011-2021)

Year	Church Planting Budget	Church Planting Missionaries	New Church Plants
2011	$24,325,678	1,429	1,003
2012	$32,452,748	Not Released	927
2013	$62,296,234	Not Released	936
2014	$61,484,579	Not Released	985
2015	$72,455,657	Not Released	926
2016	$66,859,249	Not Released	732
2017	$69,681,886	Not Released	691
2018	$68,270,217	Not Released	624

2019	$66,985,421	Not Released	552
2020	$69,478,230	Not Released	588
2021	$73,101,916	1,316	600

Source: Annuals of the SBC & 2022 SBC Book of Reports

Total Church Planting Budget 2011-2020: $667,391,815
Net Increase in SBC Churches 2011-2020: 1,850

In the ten years after GCR, NAMB spent more money ($439,943,569) on church planting but employed significantly fewer church planters and started significantly fewer new churches. More significantly, the net increase in the total number of SBC churches for the decade, was only 2,252 additional congregations after a decade. This was dramatically fewer total SBC churches than the net increase in the previous decade. Given nearly triple the budget spent, most would expect a considerably higher number than previous decades.

There has never been a decadal report weaker than the post-GCR decade in SBC history, including during the Great Depression.

Also, this smaller number of church plants may not be making as positive an impact on the future SBC as one would expect. NAMB tracks the viability of new church starts for four years. By the fourth year after their founding, more than 80% of

NAMB church plants typically continue to operate, which is a positive and encouraging survival rate. NAMB uses four years as a unit of measure because that is the length of time NAMB typically sub-

In the ten years after GCR, NAMB spent more money ($439,943,569) on church planting but employed significantly fewer church planters and started significantly fewer new churches.

sidizes a church plant and planter. What happens to those new churches after the subsidy stops? Only 65.6% of the churches started in 2014 were still active in 2019, a year after the subsidy ended. However, only 25.4% of the surviving churches were still supporting the Cooperative Program (Email from K. Ezell on June 29, 2021). Apparently, many of the new church class of 2014 still in operation after the subsidy ended appear to be drifting away from the SBC. One year does not indicate any type of trend, but this is a thread worth tracking and reporting to the SBC. The drift of new churches away from the SBC and support of the Cooperative Program could be a consequence of NAMB's strategy to connect many new churches to itself rather than seeking to root them in the SBC associations and state conventions in the region. Whether or not the present NAMB strategy is weakening the ties that bind SBC churches together is a question worth asking. The GCR task force assumed a massive increase in budget for church planting would result in a great increase in new Southern Baptist church plants. Clearly, that has not been the case.

As the momentum of decline continued to increase following the approval of GCR, concern grew slowly in the Convention. In 2017 SBC President Dr. Steve Gaines appointed a task force on how Southern Baptists could do more direct evangelism (See *The Dilemma of Decline* by Charles Kelley). That task force made very specific recommendations including a recommendation that NAMB rebuild an evangelism team, including restoring the Vice President for Evangelism position, and give increased attention to evangelism. NAMB responded positively to these recommendations, but rebuilding the culture of evangelism it once had is still a work in progress. The recent sudden departure of Evangelism VP Johnny Hunt appears to be a setback to that rebuilding process. The Senior Vice President for

---

The drift of new churches away from the SBC and support of the Cooperative Program could be a consequence of NAMB's strategy to connect many new churches to itself rather than seeking to root them in the SBC associations and state conventions in the region.

Evangelism position filled by Dr. Hunt was eliminated again. For church planting, the NAMB Send Network, has a President and Vice President. For compassion ministry, the NAMB Send Relief Network has a President. For evangelism, NAMB immediately reverted to a Senior Executive Director of Evangelism. Organizations always reflect their priorities in their flow charts. There is a bit of encouraging news. Perhaps because some public confusion followed the announcement of the hiring of Tim Dowdy as the Senior Executive Director of Evangelism to replace Hunt, who was a Senior Vice President, the Executive Director title did not last long. His title was changed in short order to Vice President for Evangelism.

All indications are that NAMB plans to continue its church planting strategy without any significant adjustments. A former NAMB Trustee told this writer that the NAMB Trustee Board had little concern about the declining statistics of the SBC because their excitement about being widely known in the evangelical world for having the "Cadillac" of church planting processes. The primary reason given for an insufficient number of church planters was the high standards NAMB requires for this "Cadillac" program. The notion that standards for church planters are so high that not enough can be found to make the strategy work would seem to indicate the need for a different strategy.

Most would agree there is a place for some form of standards in an organization seeking missionaries. The question for Southern Baptists is: What standards are necessary? Is the Convention being well-served by standards so high that not enough church planters can be found to start the necessary number of new churches for the lost of this nation to be reached? Having large amounts of money set aside to hire church planting missionaries but not enough missionary candidates to hire is a new problem in Southern Baptist life. No indications have been given that NAMB is making progress on the persistent lack of church planters. One wonders if this could be the reason NAMB refuses to report the number of church planters it has appointed. The bottom line: The North American Mission Board budgeted the money to accomplish its original goal of starting 1,500 new churches each year but cannot find the people and places on which to spend the money. There have been no reports on what NAMB does with the money it does not spend when church planting recruiting goals are not met year after year.

Regarding the question of what happened as a result of the two new ministry assignments of discipleship and leadership development, the simple answer is this: not much. In the decade that followed the GCR vote, other than absorbing the Timothy/Barnabas retreats created by Johnny

The bottom line: The North American Mission Board budgeted the money to accomplish its original goal of starting 1,500 new churches each year but cannot find the people and places on which to spend the money. There have been no reports on what NAMB does with the money it does not spend when church planting recruiting goals are not met year after year.

Hunt during his years at FBC Woodstock as they brought Pastor Hunt on board, NAMB has not announced adding a person or team to address either issue with the development of strategic plans or resources in either area for Southern Baptists to use. Associations and state conventions would be natural partners for doing leadership development with pastors in the field. Such partnerships for field-based training and pastoral support are the only way NAMB could scale up leadership development for a Convention with nearly 50,000 churches. The reluctance to develop further the partnerships it once had with associations and state conventions is and will continue to be a significant limitation of impact. It may save money, but as noted in previous charts it also reduces results. In another one of many GCR ironies, the new NAMB turned the role of directors of missions away from coaching and leadership development in order to make them church planting catalysts. Most of those were eliminated. Now it does not have a network in place for leadership development. It cannot find the necessary number of church planters.

The Timothy/Barnabas conferences were expanded in some ways, but it appears to operate on its own track for the most part. If one visits the NAMB website and clicks the button to show all available resources from NAMB, there will be very little about approaches to discipleship or leadership development. Nearly all of what is there is specifically designed for the context of church planting or church replanting. Special events are held periodically and blogs addressing each issue are posted periodically, but generally in the context of encouraging and caring for pastors rather than strategic plans and resources for churches, associations, and state conventions to develop pastors as leaders. An outside consultant in leadership was hired for about a year. He was presented as a coach for pastors, but primarily wrote a series of blogs. With nearly 50,000 churches, one leadership coach could do little else. When he departed NAMB after a brief tenure, he was not replaced for some time. Recently Dr. Ken Whitten was named as Senior Vice President for Leadership Development. How he will fulfill that role is unclear at this time.

NAMB and Lifeway Christian Resources appointed a joint task force on disciple-making in SBC churches in 2016. They produced a one-page report that was presented to the annual meeting of the SBC in 2018. Bible Engagement was identified as the most important element of disciple-making. The report to the Convention made three recommendations for enhancing disciple-making in SBC churches:

- Churches should increase the engagement of members with the Bible
- Churches should examine how to connect those who are baptized with involvement in small group discipleship
- Churches should examine the number of small groups that multiply on a regular basis.

No strategic plan or new resources for helping local churches, associations, or state conventions implement these recommendations were announced. No new staff positions to address the recommendations were created. The link for further help and resources for disciple-making has already been disabled. The whole report, brief as it was, was more closely tied to the "*Replicate Ministry*" of chairman Dr. Robbie Gallaty than it was to either Lifeway or NAMB.

The pattern of NAMB has been very consistent during the post-GCR decade. In nearly every report he makes to the SBC, the president says NAMB has two primary points of focus: church planting (Send Network) and compassion ministry (Send Relief). He means it. When Southern Baptists ask NAMB to do other things, such as evangelism or discipleship, the response bears more resemblance to a patchwork quilt than a strategic plan scaled for 50,000 churches and supported by staff and budget over a prolonged period of time. Field support for anything other than church planting or compassion ministry is very limited. Little to nothing is done to help state conventions and associations assist churches in addressing such issues. The typical way NAMB addresses issues other than church planting and compassion ministry is with blogs, occasional conferences, and free resources for pastors, along with part-time consultants or advocates.

The standard practice for NAMB since its inception was to report in the *SBC Annual* each year what work its employees were assigned to do. Present NAMB leadership eliminated that report. Southern Baptists are not told how many NAMB employees or missionaries are assigned to any area of work. It is a mystery. Virtually all Director of Mission positions NAMB funded with the state conventions have been eliminated, as have many of the church planting catalysts. Neither the number of appointed missionaries assigned to church planting nor the missionaries assigned to other tasks is reported. A new type of worker called an ambassador has been added to employee categories. Some ambassadors who appear to do the kind of work the typical Director of Missions did are assigned to the territory of state conventions, but totally under control of NAMB. Others appear to be primarily good will ambassadors encouraging positive attitudes toward the Board. Their numbers appear to be large, but neither their numbers nor their exact job descriptions are reported to the SBC or to the state conventions in the areas where they serve. The post-GCR NAMB is far and away the least transparent, least open entity in the SBC.

The Great Commission Resurgence task force wanted a very different NAMB, and they got it. Being different would not be a problem if the Convention and its churches were thriving as a result. Unfortunately, the decline that started before the Great Commission Resurgence, accelerated even further after NAMB embraced its recommendations. Component Four is the heart of the GCR proposals, and that heart is not healthy. SBC statistics and the agenda at SBC annual meetings in recent years indicate that the churches of the SBC are turning away from the Great Commission and not towards it. The

The post-GCR NAMB is far and away the least transparent, least open entity in the SBC.

significant reduction in funding for state conventions and associations combined with efforts to change the role of Directors of Missions from coaching and supporting the churches in an area to the role of church planting catalysts focused intensely on starting new churches has diminished the support systems available to pastors and churches, especially outside the

Unfortunately, the decline that started before the Great Commission Resurgence, accelerated even further after NAMB embraced its recommendations.

stronger state conventions in the South. Of great concern are the indications that NAMB's strategic plans are tearing away at the fabric of cooperation that has been a major distinctive of Southern Baptists since they first came together to form the Southern Baptist Convention. When entire state conventions begin to discuss opting out of the Cooperative Program as it is designed, previously unthinkable futures for the SBC could emerge.

The Home Mission Board/North American Mission Board was a critical driver for explosive expansion during the years of greatest growth for the Convention's churches. More than any other SBC entity, it appears to be a critical driver in this era of historic, unprecedented decline. No other administration of HMB/NAMB has spent so much money and had such little positive effect on measurable outcomes in SBC churches. Southern Baptists should ask if this is what they want in a North American Mission Board.

_____

The Home Mission Board/ North American Mission Board was a critical driver for explosive expansion during the years of greatest growth for the Convention's churches. More than any other SBC entity, it appears to be a critical driver in this era of historic, unprecedented decline. No other administration of HMB/NAMB has spent so much money and had such little positive effect on measurable outcomes in SBC churches.

_____

A healthy SBC should never wonder whether or not NAMB or any SBC entity should try new ways to accomplish its mission. The right to do so is a given for any organization that wants to thrive over time. On the other hand, a healthy SBC must always ask, after a reasonable time, if a new strategy or new approach worked.

Charles S. Kelley Jr.

Component Five: Reaching Unreached and Underserved People Groups Within North America

Component Five turns to the International Mission Board for a minor tweak in its relationship with the North American Mission Board. Both have had a focus on Unreached and Underserved people groups in recent years. The GCR Task Force wanted to put a gate in the fence separating North America from the rest of the world. It asked that IMB missionaries working with specific people groups overseas be allowed to work in US cities to reach those people groups when requested to do so by NAMB. This was viewed by the Convention as a reasonable exception to the specific territorial limitations assigned to the two entities. Given the different organizational cultures of the two Boards, they agreed with the change but have not actively sought engagement.

We ask Southern Baptists to entrust to the International Mission Board the ministry of reaching unreached and underserved people groups without regard to any geographic limitation (2010 SBC Annual, p.85).

The Southern Baptist Convention has an old and carefully observed requirement for SBC entities to stay within their assigned lanes, not working against each other or working in overlapping areas of mission. Maintaining an exclusive focus on their specific assignments was viewed as particularly important for the International Mission Board (IMB) and the North American Mission Board. The purpose of this recommendation was not to blur the lines between the different missions of the two boards but to allow NAMB to tap into the expertise of the IMB in order to better reach international populations very familiar to the international missionaries of Southern Baptists, but now living in American cities and colleges. This issue does not appear to have been raised by a request from either mission board. Apparently, the issue was a concern that originated with the task force. NAMB had incorporated the people group language in its founding documents, seeking to start congregations among all people groups located in North America (*1995 SBC Annual*, p. 167). This was not a call for NAMB to address a new need.

Apparently, the task force envisioned more than just consultative work to help NAMB personnel and teams know how to reach unreached and underserved people groups within North America. They wanted IMB personnel to be free to be involved in conducting church planting and mission activities targeting unreached people groups whose origins were overseas, within North America in the place of or alongside NAMB personnel. Doing this kind of consultative work and direct mission activity on a regular basis within North America would require an adjustment to the ministry assignment of the IMB, and that adjustment would have to be approved by the SBC. The task force made it very clear that this recommendation had been made after "thorough consideration" with NAMB leadership. They did not mention "thorough consideration" with IMB leadership.

Following the approval of the GCR proposals, actions to adjust SBC ministry assignments and make this recommendation happen were taken and submitted to the next meeting of the Southern Baptist Convention. The adjustments garnered easy approval without discussion. The IMB is now allowed to work with unreached and underserved people groups within the United States and Canada.

WHAT HAPPENED?

The mission boards treated this revised strategy as more of a technical adjustment than groundbreaking change. The task force did note at the end of its recommendation that a "spirit of cooperation" between the boards on this issue did already exist. Under the leadership of IMB presidents Jerry Rankin and Tom Eliff, Southern Baptists were encouraged to think of the lost world in terms of people groups rather than nations. Instead of taking the Gospel to this nation or that nation, Southern Baptists often heard about getting the Gospel to various people groups who could be found in many different nations, including the United States. At its founding the first NAMB ministry referred to starting churches "among all people groups." (1995 SBC Annual, p.167). The presidents who served NAMB would regularly refer to their work with unreached and underserved populations and in unreached and underserved areas of North America. The idea of IMB personnel starting churches in North America was new, but having an intentional overlap to reach international populations living in North America was not.

Both boards immediately acted to propose the recommended changes in ministry assignment to the SBC. With little explanation from the entity heads, the SBC acted to approve the changes without discussion or comment at the next annual meeting in 2011. Clearly this move was not viewed as a controversial or groundbreaking move by most Southern Baptists before, during, or after the Convention meeting. Perhaps this can be attributed to a general recognition that the world has become a global community more than a collection of nations. Most surprising is the lack of reference by either NAMB or IMB to IMB work in North American cities or campuses in the years since GCR was passed and the ministry assignment changes were made. Whatever has happened in this area in the intervening years of the post-GCR decade did not warrant enough attention to be made a focal point in the annual SBC reports of either entity. It is not "bragging material" to be called to the attention of SBC messengers or churches. The IMB reports on international ministry and NAMB reports on North American ministry as they always have. An insider from one of the Boards offered a bit more perspective. The internal culture of the two Boards is different. Working together on occasion was always a bit stiff and unnatural. The GCR proposal did not change those dynamics. Southern Baptists are not likely to hear much news on this front in the future. What is possible is not always likely to be actionable.

Recently NAMB and IMB have used the ministry assignment changes to form a different agreement on joint efforts in Send Relief, allowing NAMB to work overseas and mobilize churches to work overseas in compassion ministry and disaster relief. This joint effort in compassion ministry has elicited more attention from both entities than did the GCR recommendation regarding taking the gospel to and planting churches for unreached people groups in

North America. This component did not make a big splash, nor did it do any harm. It rarely surfaces in SBC conversations. Related developments are unlikely to find a place in reports from either president unless it is in the area of Send Relief issues.

Charles S. Kelley Jr.

Component Six: Promoting CP and Elevating Stewardship

omponent Six returns attention to the Cooperative Program, specifically recommending
how to increase support for it. Apparently, it is an
attempt to tweak an adjustment made in the Covenant for a New Century that did not work out as
planned. It recognizes and affirms the essential role
in CP promotion that state conventions must play.

*We strongly encourage the Executive Committee of
the Southern Baptist Convention to work with the state
conventions, charged with the responsibility of Cooperative Program and stewardship education, in developing a
strategy for encouraging our churches to greater participation and investment in the Cooperative Program*

*Our hope is that a unified strategy with clearly estab-
lished goals will be in place by the meeting of the Southern
Baptist Convention in 2013 (2010 SBC Annual p. 85)*

This proposal was the second of the seven components to address the Cooperative Program. The
primary focus of Component Three was the eleva-
tion of designated giving (Great Commission Giv-

ing) to the same level of recognition and praise for the Cooperative Program. Component Six, however, has the sole purpose of promoting CP giving. It appears to be an attempt to address a miscalculation from the Covenant for a New Century, which was a massive effort to restructure the SBC in 1995.

The SBC Executive Committee initiated a task force in 1995 to consider downsizing the number of Convention entities and reassigning some historic responsibilities to streamline the Convention for the future. When the Convention leaders who emerged during the Conservative Resurgence began to consider what the future held for a newly energized SBC, many felt reducing the denominational bureaucracy and the assignments of various responsibilities in terms of efficiencies rather than precedent, would position the Convention for a maximum investment in missions and ministry. Southern Baptists hoped it would also help the Convention avoid the mistakes of other denominations who waited until sinking financial realities compelled such reductions.

One of the recommendations made by that task force was to eliminate the SBC Stewardship Commission, which promoted stewardship in general and Cooperative Program giving in particular, and give the Executive Committee primary responsibility for Cooperative Program promotion and, later on, stewardship promotion. It is likely this adjustment was also an effort to give the SBC itself a larger role in CP promotion. When the Cooperative Program was created in 1925, by design the state conventions were given the primary role in CP promotion. Many of the state conventions were overtly or tacitly opposed to the Conservative Resurgence (CR). The success of the Conservative Resurgence brought a new generation of outsiders into positions of SBC leadership. Tensions from the Resurgence remained, fraying some relationships between the new SBC leaders and many convention leaders.

For many years, the annual meeting of state conventions included reports from most SBC entities. The six seminary presidents devised a schedule that rotated them across the nation. Each state convention would hear from one seminary each year and every seminary at least once every six years. All the entity heads and some of their key leaders were on the road every fall for those state meetings, creating an exhaustive schedule. There would usually be a brief report to the Convention, some mix- and-mingle time with the Baptists who attended, and often a luncheon or breakfast with those interested in knowing more. It was part of the fabric holding the SBC family together and reminding each other regularly of the scale of the Southern Baptist Convention's size and scope. If you attended your state convention meeting, you could meet and talk to one or more entity heads. Entity heads could hear directly from people in the pews. In every presentation, most entity heads would thank those present for their support of the Cooperative Program and remind them what it was and why it mattered. The process was consuming for entity leaders, but it was part of the CP promotion process, a part that has largely disappeared.

As tensions from the Conservative Resurgence at the national SBC level spilled over into state conventions, the invitations to state conventions for entity heads began to dwindle. At the same time there was a movement toward shorter convention meetings at both state and national levels. The combination of those tensions eroded the practice of entity reports significantly. The easiest way to make a state convention shorter was to eliminate the slot for guests from far away. Today most entity heads visit a fraction of the conventions they once attended.

One dynamic apparently at play in the Covenant for a New Century was an interest by some in the SBC in gaining more influence and control over things that affected the whole SBC. Nothing was of greater significance than CP, the lifeblood of SBC ministries. Magnifying the role of the Executive Committee in CP promotion looked like one way for the new generation of SBC leaders to get more involved in an important area. It turned out that the promotion of CP giving was more complex and difficult than expected. By 2010, all indications were that the Cooperative Program was facing real challenges, and the Executive Committee alone was unlikely to be able to overcome the headwinds. The Covenant for a New Century plan apparently did not produce the desired fundraising results. This proposal was in effect a strategic adjustment to the actions of 1995. Southern Baptists tried something new. It did not work as expected. They knew adjustments were needed. The importance of state conventions in the CP process had become more obvious.

GCR Chairman Floyd acknowledged the need for the state conventions to take the lead in both CP promotion and stewardship education. After noting Albert McClellan's documentation that CP was created with the understanding that state conventions should be responsible for promoting CP among the churches and gathering CP from the churches, Floyd asserted:

> The reason for this is straightforward and easy to see. The state conventions have the mechanisms in place to collect funds and promote the Cooperative Program. This has been their historic role and continuing passion. (*2010 SBC Annual*, p. 86)

The Task Force did not intend for the Executive Committee to pull away from CP promotion. What they envisioned was an active strategic partnership in which both the state conventions and the

Executive Committee were coordinating efforts to enhance participation in CP giving and the amount of money raised each year. The formal recommendation from the task force was that a unified strategy involving both the state conventions and the EC would be in place by the 2013 meeting of the SBC. They also asked that the unified strategy include clear, specific goals.

The context of this recommendation for increased involvement of the state conventions in CP promotion is worth noting. In his original chapel address calling for a Great Commission Resurgence, Dr. Daniel Akin referred to the state conventions as "bloated bureaucracies" hindering SBC efforts to fulfill the Great Commission. In Component Three, the state conventions were asked to increase the percentage of CP funds being forwarded to the Southern Baptist Convention, which would likely mean a reduction in their annual budgets. In Component Four the task force recommended NAMB end all Cooperative Agreements with the state conventions, weakening significantly their partnerships with NAMB and further reducing their budgets. In effect the task force was asking the state conventions to set aside concerns about internal and external pressures likely to limit their budgets in order to raise more for the national convention. The benefit for adopting this resolution for the SBC was clear. For the state conventions the benefit was not so obvious. In another GCR irony, this recommendation acknowledged that the state conventions did play a crucial role in the SBC universe.

In effect the task force was asking the state conventions to set aside concerns about internal and external pressures likely to limit their budgets in order to raise more for the national convention. The benefit for adopting this resolution for the SBC was clear. For the state conventions the benefit was not so obvious. In another GCR irony, this recommendation acknowledged that the state conventions did play a crucial role in the SBC universe.

There was no discussion on this component when the GCR proposals were brought to the floor of the Convention. The only concerns raised about it prior to the Convention came from state convention voices. Component Three and Component Four were of far greater concern. There was virtually no discussion on what an enhanced partnership on CP promotion between the EC and the state conventions might look like. Component Six was easily passed.

WHAT HAPPENED?

The GCR target of having a unified strategy for Cooperative Program promotion with clearly established goals coming jointly from the EC and the state conventions in place by the 2013 meeting of the Southern Baptist Convention was modest in its results. Frank Page was a member of the GCR Task Force and became the CEO of the Executive Committee shortly after the GCR proposals were approved. He was widely known as an aggressive supporter of the Cooperative Program. As CEO of the Executive Committee, Page was intentional and aggressive in promoting the Cooperative Program and in building cooperative relationships with the state conventions throughout his tenure. As a pastor he had been very supportive of the Cooperative Program. Most felt his active and consistent work to lead the churches he served to support CP played a key role in his election as SBC President. Under his leadership, the EC did launch an initiative called "Great Commission Advance" that included a clear emphasis on CP. The initial launch did take place at the 2013 SBC annual meeting, with the comprehensive launch coming in 2014. As a backdrop the Convention program was filled with videos promoting CP and highlighting its impact on people and ministries. Churches were challenged to give 1 % more to CP each year for ten years as a lead into the 100th anniversary of CP in 2025. In his announcement of the campaign, Page noted that it was being undertaken with state convention and entity partnerships (*Baptist Press*, Sept. 22, 2015). Although the GCR recommendations were not mentioned by Page or the EC in conjunction with the Great Commission Advance campaign, it seems fair to assume the emphasis was the response to this recommendation from the task force.

As noted in the discussion of Component Three and Great Commission giving, the decade following the approval of GCR by the Convention was historically weak, losing ground that the SBC is far from recovering. Undesignated giving to their churches by Southern Baptists did not drop as much as money given to the SBC by the churches, but congregational giving remained flat for the decade. The Southern Baptist Convention, the state conventions, and SBC churches face growing, significant fiscal challenges.

Decadal Percentage Changes in SBC Giving
(1970-2021)

Years	Total Receipts by SBC Churches	Total of Undesignated Gifts to SBC Churches	Total CP Gifts from SBC Churches	SBC Share of Total CP	Total CP as % of Undesignated Gifts
1970s	9.94%	NA	8.97%	34.41%	N/A
1980s	7.58%	5.10%	6.83%	37.47%	10.50%
1990s	5.42%	4.91%	2.68%	37.04%	8.73%
2000s	4.12%	4.82%	2.23%	37.16%	6.80%
2010s	(0.21%)	0.71%	(1.16%)	39.34%	5.22%
Last 5 Yrs	0.65%	1.20%	(0.73%)	41.27%	4.79%

Chart prepared from the Southern Baptist Convention Annual of 2019 and Book of Reports, 2022

The trend of decline in giving is clear. The only upward trend is in the SBC share of total CP income. That upward movement reflects a change in the allocation process, not the income stream for the Cooperative Program. If the total CP income were like a pie, the SBC share of CP is a slice of that pie. The slice of the pie is getting bigger, but the pie itself is getting smaller. The slice of the pie may be bigger, but it does not mean SBC entities are receiving more money.

One of the most concerning CP trends is rarely discussed and apparently not consistently tracked. Giving to CP is necessary for a church to send messengers to annual Convention meetings. Giving to CP is necessary to become a SBC church. Many Southern Baptists may not realize giving to CP is not necessary to remain a SBC church once you have become a member. The SBC Executive Committee published an eye-opening chart in the Summer 2021 edition of *SBC Life Journal*. It tracked the giving of SBC churches to CP since the approval of GCR in 2010. The chart below reveals what I believe to be one of the most troubling trends reflecting a potential emerging future for the SBC.

If the total CP income were like a pie, the SBC share of CP is a slice of that pie. The slice of the pie is getting bigger, but the pie itself is getting smaller. The slice of the pie may be bigger, but it does not mean SBC entities are receiving more money.

Non-CP Churches in the SBC (2010-2021)

Year	Total SBC Churches	Non-CP SBC Churches	% of Non-CP SBC Churches
2010	46,640	13,897	29.79%
2011	46,410	16,134	34.76%
2012	46,713	16,493	35.30%

2013	46,877	16,692	36.60%
2014	48,147	18,675	38.78%
2015	47,746	18,220	38.16%
2016	48,265	18,151	37.60%
2017	48,585	18,931	38.96%
2018	48,494	18,996	39.17%
2019	48,709	19,645	40.33%
2020			
2021			

Data from SBC Life Journal, Summer 2021 and Annuals of the Southern Baptist Convention

The Convention seems to be facing a steady increase in the number of SBC churches who are not giving a dime to the Cooperative Program. That trend continued unabated following the GCR approval. 13,897 SBC churches did not give anything through CP in 2010. By 2019, the last year for which numbers are available at the time of this report, 19,645 churches, which is about 40% of all SBC churches did not give to the Cooperative Program. Far from being mobilized in their support of SBC Great Commission efforts, 5,748 SBC churches opted out of CP support after the GCR proposals were approved (*SBC Life Journal, Summer 2021*, p. 9). This could be fallout from the creation of Great Commission Giving.

Clearly, the last decade has demonstrated that Southern Baptists have a serious stewardship problem. More specifically Southern Baptists have a CP support problem. Just as clearly, the Great Commission Resurgence did not produce a solution. In fact, the problem increased. As of this writing, the updated numbers on how many SBC churches gave to CP and how many did not give to CP since 2019 have not yet been released. When asked for an update, the EC staff reported that they do not have the numbers. That lack of updated data is troubling in a different way. Apparently, the numbers on how many churches are not giving to CP are no longer being actively tracked.

More specifically Southern Baptists have a CP support problem. Just as clearly, the Great Commission Resurgence did not produce a solution. In fact, the problem increased.

Component Seven: The Calling of the Nations and the SBC Allocation Budget

Component Seven returns attention to the International Mission Board. It is a recommendation to increase the Cooperative Program allocation for the IMB by one percent and to reduce the allocation for Facilitating Ministries (the Executive Committee) by one point. Giving more money for International Missions is always a good close for a Southern Baptist audience.

We ask that the Cooperative Program SBC Allocation Budget percentage received by the International Mission Board be raised to 51%

We further ask that this increase be funded by a similar reduction in the budget granted to Facilitating Ministries (2010 SBC Annual, p.85)

One result of the Covenant for a New Century in 1995 was an increase of the percentage of the SBC Cooperative Program distribution going to the International Mission Board to 50%. The GCR task force felt the time had come to give the IMB

51% of national CP funds. No mention was made that overall CP income continued to fall from its 2007 high.

Without question the historic priority of Southern Baptists is missions, especially international missions. The determination to take a cooperative approach to reaching the world for Christ was one of the major factors in the creation of the SBC. the first creative act of the Convention was the establishment of a Board for Foreign Missions. Thus, a recommendation to increase the money spent on international missions had not a hint of controversy in pre-Convention social media and conversations. It was not mentioned in the discussion when the GCR proposals were under consideration by Convention messengers. The retiring EC president was not a fan of the money coming solely from the EC budget, but his limited concern had no traction with Southern Baptists. Some advocated an even larger increase made possible by reducing the allocation for theological education. This was opposed by the president of the IMB along with many others and generated little interest or comment. In the absence of controversy, steps were taken to adjust the CP distribution to the IMB as requested as soon as the SBC budget processes allowed.

What Happened?

The increased CP budget allocation was important for the IMB, but perhaps not in the way envisioned by the task force. It did not raise missions funding to new levels, but it did offer some protection to the IMB budget as CP giving continued a prolonged slide. From a total Cooperative Program giving of $548 million in 2008, income fell to a low of $462.3 million in 2019, before the pandemic. In 2021, the total CP was $457,928,996. The SBC portion of CP was increased by many state conventions, but it was an increase coming out of a declining total. In the same way, the IMB slice of the CP allocation pie was larger, but it was a larger piece of a smaller pie. In spite of a larger percentage of CP going to the SBC and a larger percentage of the SBC CP going to the IMB, it has yet to return to the IMB 2007 CP allocation of $102 million. The 2021 CP allocation for the IMB was $96,823,210. The increase in the budget allocation for the IMB by GCR did not actually increase the amount of CP for the Board. The benefit of the allocation increase, however, was quite real. It kept the IMB allocation from falling as much as it otherwise would have fallen. In spite of the focus of GCR on improving the funding of the Great Commission, the expected improvement did not happen. The steadily increasing CP giving that was happening prior to 2008 and the Great Recession, did not return after GCR. The trend of smaller increases for CP giving turned into actual decline.

What Southern Baptists today are giving to their churches and what their churches are giving to the Cooperative Program are matters of profound concern for the future of the SBC.

The steadily increasing CP giving that was happening prior to 2008 and the Great Recession, did not return after GCR. The trend of smaller increases for CP giving turned into actual decline.

Miscellaneous Matters

Following the formal proposals made to the Convention, the task force included lists of challenges for Southern Baptists to consider as means to enhance the Great Commission impact of the Convention and its churches. These challenges were arranged in categories including from one to more than thirty suggestions for each area. The categories for these challenges included individual Christians, individual families, local churches and pastors, local associations, state conventions, SBC entities, and all SBC leaders. No responsibility was assigned to encourage efforts to fulfill the responsibilities listed or to report back to the SBC on what efforts were made to implement them. Apparently, the assumption was that challenges read into the record of the SBC would be embraced and implemented by those to whom they were addressed. Some dates and some specific targets were included in various parts of the GCR proposals, but no framework for progress reports on the proposals was included for Convention action. Some proposals requiring action by an entity were acted upon and reported to the 2011 SBC. Others were not. The dozens of challenges included in the postscript of the GCR report were largely ignored by the SBC, its entities, and its churches. There were too many suggestions covering too broad and diverse a target audience to ever be taken seriously, or even to become known, in such a loosely organized family of churches. In this case, less would have been more. The list of challenges to the various publics forming the SBC were essentially a postscript to the GCR proposals for those who were interested enough to wade through them. As such they were inconsequential in terms of the Great Commission activities and productivity of Southern Baptists.

Part Three:

Reflections

Charles S. Kelley Jr.

Summary

After receiving permission from the 2009 Southern Baptist Convention, SBC President Johnny Hunt appointed a Great Commission Resurgence Task Force, hoping to have a similar impact in SBC life as that which came through the deeply transforming movement known as the Conservative Resurgence. The task force met during the months that followed their appointment to discuss how to ignite a fresh passion for the Great Commission among Southern Baptists. The task force brought its report and recommendations to the 2010 meeting of the SBC in Orlando, the same Convention site that in 2000 hosted the culmination of the Conservative Resurgence in the overwhelming approval of the *Baptist Faith and Message 2000*.

After giving brief attention to the urgency of the Great Commission, the need for greater financial support for Great Commission ministries, and some comments on a Great Commission theology, the task force identified seven basic components giving rise to a number of recommendations on how to stimulate a Great Commission Resurgence. The proposals included recommendations for:

- The approval of official SBC vision and values statements

- The affirmation of a designated giving option to be known as Great Commission Giving in addition to an affirmation of the Cooperative Program
- The restructuring of the relationship between the North American Mission Board and the state conventions
- A massive shift of funding and emphasis from evangelism to church planting
- Encouragement for the International Mission Board to be allowed to work with unreached people groups in the United States
- A suggestion to increase the allocation for the IMB in the SBC budget
- A call for state conventions to increase the funds they gave to the national CP, to take the point in the promotion of Cooperative Program giving within their states, and to give up stable funding they received for decades from NAMB for shared ministries

A very long list of various Great Commission challenges was issued to all Southern Baptist people and ministries as a postscript to close the report.

In spite of the best intentions of President Hunt and the task force he appointed, the Great Commission Resurgence proposals proved to be a Great Commission Regression. Baptisms dropped to levels not seen since the 1930s. After starting 1,003 new churches in 2011, the number of new church plants dropped nearly 50% in the next ten years, in spite of massive increases in the budget for and promotion of church planting at the North American Mission Board. The support of NAMB for state conventions in the most unchurched regions of the country dropped dramatically, creating unprecedented tensions yet to be resolved. Both mission boards experienced a significant decline in the number of missionaries under appointment. The giving of Southern Baptists to their churches and of SBC churches to the Cooperative Program continued a downward slide.

> *In spite of the best intentions . . . the Great Commission Resurgence proposals proved to be a Great Commission Regression. Baptisms dropped to levels not seen since the 1930s. . . After starting 1,003 new churches in 2011, the number of new church plants dropped nearly 50% in the next ten years, in spite of massive increases in the budget for and promotion of church planting at the North American Mission Board.*

Many state conventions did forward more of their CP money to the national CP, but declining CP support from SBC churches meant the increase was merely a larger slice of a smaller pie, not additional money flowing into Southern Baptist coffers at a higher rate. 2007 still marks the record year for the SBC portion of the Cooperative Program, and that record has not been matched in the post-GCR era. By 2021, both the state and the SBC Cooperative Program budgets were smaller than they were in 2010, the year GCR was approved. The percentage of the undesignated gifts received by SBC churches that were then given by those churches to the Cooperative Program declined steadily during the decade. Most concerning, by 2019 approximately 40% of SBC churches did not give a dime to the Cooperative Program.

The support of NAMB for state conventions in the most unchurched regions of the country dropped dramatically, creating unprecedented tensions yet to be resolved. Both mission boards experienced a significant decline in the number of missionaries under appointment. The giving of Southern Baptists to their churches and of SBC churches to the Cooperative Program continued a downward slide.

The decade following GCR approval saw the worst statistical decline in one decade in SBC history. Membership, baptisms per church, worship attendance, church plants, missionaries, CP giving, and Great Commission Giving–the new giving category created by GCR to track all forms of giving in SBC life–were all down across the board. The SBC was in the early years of an era of decline when the GCR proposals were adopted. That decline accelerated following the approval of those proposals. By any standard of measure, the Great Commission Resurgence was merely a moment, not a movement in Southern Baptist life.

A decade after GCR, Southern Baptists find themselves mired in the deepest crisis they have faced since the Civil War threatened their very existence. To be sure, this is not a crisis of survival. Almost certainly the SBC will go far into the future. This is a crisis of church health, of fruitfulness, and of continuing Great Commission significance. If the crisis continues unabated, how will the missionary enterprise of Southern Baptists, recognized by all as the crown jewel of the SBC since the Convention began in 1845, be affected? Undoubtedly, the Gospel

> *The SBC was in the early years of an era of decline when the GCR proposals were adopted. That decline accelerated following the approval of those proposals. By any standard of measure, the Great Commission Resurgence was merely a moment, not a movement in Southern Baptist life.*

will continue to advance. The Kingdom of God will continue to grow. But will Southern Baptists remain in the vanguard of that advance? Such a thought was unthinkable in the past. It is not unthinkable today.

Lessons Learned from the Great Commission Resurgence

There can be no question or debate about the need for a Great Commission Resurgence across the Southern Baptist Convention today. In 2010, the Southern Baptist Convention attempted to start one. A decade has passed, and the results are in. SBC churches as a body have never been more inefficient and unfruitful in reaching the lost living in their communities than they are now. The need for a Great Commission Resurgence is even greater today. How can a Great Commission Resurgence get started? The GCR Task Force attempted to answer that question in 2010. Ten years later it is clear that those proposals did not achieve the expected results.

Having examined the proposals and the outcomes that resulted, the next question is: What did Southern Baptists learn from the outcomes of the Great Commission Resurgence proposals?

A decade has passed, and the results are in. SBC churches as a body have never been more inefficient and unfruitful in reaching the lost living in their communities than they are now.

LESSON ONE:
THERE ARE NO SHORTCUTS ON THE ROAD TO DEEP INFLUENCE

The Great Commission Resurgence is a perfect illustration of the difference between a moment and a movement. The Conservative Resurgence inspired the name of the Great Commission Resurgence. It turned the SBC away from a theological drift to the left and toward a wholehearted embrace of the divine inspiration of Scripture and traditional Baptist theology. Four decades later it continues to exert a profound theological influence on the SBC. The Great Commission Resurgence was more like a moment that held the attention of the Convention for about two years before fading away from SBC conversations rather quickly. There is little evidence of enhanced engagement by Southern Baptist churches in fulfilling the Great Commission in the nation and world, nor is there widespread concern and conversation about the deepening decline of the SBC and its churches as Great Commission interest waned.

A key difference between the Conservative Resurgence and the Great Commission Resurgence approaches to change was the intent and strategy of leadership.

Leaders of the Conservative Resurgence planned to sustain the attention of the SBC for at least a decade on the problem of liberal theology and a solution to that problem. The agenda was simple. A clear problem and a clear solution that could be easily explained from a platform, over lunch, or in conversations. The issue of a return to the Bible was identified and publicized before Adrian Rog-

A key difference between the Conservative Resurgence and the Great Commission Resurgence approaches to change was the intent and strategy of leadership.

ers was elected in 1979. He was elected in order to address that issue and knew before the votes were counted what he would do if elected. He also knew an all-out effort to elect other presidents to carry on the battle he started would follow his tenure. The issue chose the President during those years rather than the President choosing the issue he wanted to address. With each passing year, more and more was done to educate Southern Baptists about the problem of liberal theology and enlist their involvement in implementing a solution to that problem. Pastors Conferences, town hall meetings, regional Bible conferences, newsletters, and other print projects and uncountable numbers of phone calls and conversations were the primary means of communication in the days before the internet and social media. All of them emphasized the annual meeting of the SBC was the gathering point to address this problem in a transformative way. The election of consecutive SBC presidents and the resulting appointment of conservative Trustees to entity boards were the primary solutions. The election of Rogers in 1979 was always intended to be the launching of a prolonged movement.

By contrast, various leaders and friends came together in the months after President Hunt was elected and together with him discussed

> *The issue chose the President during those years rather than the President choosing the issue he wanted to address.*

what he could address during his two-year presidency. The public focus chosen for emphasis was an indirect approach to the Great Commission that would center on internal SBC issues of funding distribution, denominational relationships, and a strategic shift from evangelism to church planting. This indirect approach was in contrast to a direct approach that would have attempted to mobilize SBC churches for immediate engagement in Great Commission activities. For implementation of this agenda those who drove GCR focused attention and efforts on two annual meetings of the SBC. The first would target securing permission for Hunt to appoint a Great Commission Resurgence Task Force. The second would target getting approval of the task force report and recommendations. A task force of twenty-three (including Hunt) were the "soldiers" in the GCR initiative as opposed to the thousands of Southern Baptists enlisted in the Conservative Resurgence for specific actions. The task force members were charged with creating recommendations rather than taking action.

Other than social media blogs, BP stories and a single textbook-style academic book (*The Great Commission Resurgence: Fulfilling God's Mandate In Our Time*, edited by Lawless and Greenway), no apparent plans were made to keep the GCR discussion alive and push the promotion of and discussion about a Great Commission Resurgence to more and more pastors, lay leaders and churches after the 2010 Convention closed. When little fresh fuel was added to the fire after 2010, the GCR discussion faded away. Instead, a new SBC President was elected at that 2010 Convention, and, as usual, the SBC moved on. "What can I do during my two-year tenure as SBC President?" is one question. "How can I make a deep impact on the Great Commission engagement of the Southern Baptist Convention?" is quite a different question. The Conservative Resurgence was a movement. The Great Commission Resurgence was a moment.

LESSON TWO:
USING THE TERM "GREAT COMMISSION" IS NOT GREAT COMMISSION ENGAGEMENT

The Great Commission Resurgence task force chose to give its attention to SBC funding distribution and Convention infrastructure rather than mobilizing Southern Baptists and their churches to reach the lost in their communities and disciple those they reached. The "small print" in the introduction and conclusion of the document indicates the committee had some awareness of the historic evangelistic crisis facing SBC churches; but calling for greater evangelistic engagement by Southern Baptists and calling for the North American Mission Board to take actions that would increase evangelistic activities in churches in order to reach more of the lost living around them was not on the task force agenda. Clearly the task force had an agenda, but it was not "preachable," meaning not easily transferable among Southern Baptists. Few would describe infrastructure and funding issues as pillars of the Great Commission that would draw a hearty "Amen" from Convention pulpits or pews.

The decision to recommend an official endorsement of designated giving as a way to recognize and celebrate pastors and churches giving minimal support to CP was instantly perceived by a great many Southern Baptists as the creation of a competitor to the Cooperative Program, the lifeblood of all SBC ministry outside of the local church. The idea of Great Commission Giving took all of the oxygen out of the room for conversations about actual Great Commission challenges and activities in Southern Baptist life. Nearly all of the pre-Convention GCR conversations, the GCR discussion in the Convention, and the post-Convention GCR reflections were exclusively about Great Commission Giving versus Cooperative Program Giving. The conversation Southern Baptists could have had and needed to have was about the historic, profound evangelism crisis facing most SBC churches and how that crisis could be overcome. Unfortunately, that true Great Commission conversation was aborted when Great Commission Giving took the stage. The fact that the SBC had a focus on a Great Commission Resurgence without ever addressing the state of Great Commission activity in SBC

The conversation Southern Baptists could have had and needed to have was about the historic, profound evangelism crisis facing most SBC churches and how that crisis could be overcome. Unfortunately, that true Great Commission conversation was aborted when Great Commission Giving took the stage.

churches is perhaps the saddest legacy of GCR. We really needed that true Great Commission conversation. A decade has passed, and we still have not had that conversation. According to statistics from the Executive Committee shared above, in 2010 29.79% of SBC churches did not give to CP. By 2019, 40.33% of SBC churches did not give to CP. All the time and energy spent on financial conversations did not strengthen financial support for the Great Commission. It weakened further what was already in decline.

LESSON THREE:
BEING OBLIVIOUS TO THE OBVIOUS RARELY ENDS WELL

Johnny Hunt was elected President of the SBC at the annual meeting of the SBC in 2008. At that same Convention, in his report to the messengers NAMB President Geoffery Hammond called for a Great Commission Resurgence and announced NAMB was planning a massive evangelism initiative with the intent of sharing the Gospel with every person in the United States by 2020. At the 2009 annual meeting, the SBC gave President Hunt the approval to appoint a Great Commission Resurgence Task Force. At that same Convention, NAMB announced every state convention and many associations had agreed to participate in and support the *God's Plan for Shar-*

ing (GPS) initiative to mobilize Southern Baptists to share the Gospel with every person in America by 2020. It would incorporate a variety of approaches for evangelism, beginning with a national prayer movement and provide a plan to layer in various approaches to sharing the Gospel year by year for a decade, gathering momentum year by year with the hope that by 2020 every person in North America would hear the Gospel and have an opportunity to be saved. In the annual SBC meeting of 2010, the year the GCR proposals were recommended and approved, NAMB announced to Convention messengers that all strategies and resources for the *God's Plan for Sharing* initiative had been field-tested and approved, Convention-wide partnerships had been secured, and the launch of the most massive effort in SBC history to make Christ known to all was officially underway. What could be more ideal than calling for a Great Commission Resurgence as the most massive evangelistic initiative in the history of the SBC was launched?

Unfortunately, the *God's Plan for Sharing* initiative was completely ignored by the GCR task force. In spite of all the time, energy, and money already spent to mobilize the entire SBC in a fresh engagement with the Great Commission year by year for a decade, the GPS initiative did not merit a passing reference in the GCR proposals. Early announcement of the Great Commission Giving proposal was widely viewed as the creation of a competitor to the Cooperative Program. The threat of the potential effect of that action on CP giving took all the oxygen out of any discussion about evangelism, including the promotion of the *God's Plan for Sharing* initiative before, during, and after the 2010 SBC annual meeting. The GCR recommendations to reduce state convention budgets, end the Cooperative Agreements between the state conventions and NAMB, and shift attention from evangelism to church planting disrupted all the SBC partnerships that had been put together so carefully to make Great Commission activities the focal point of SBC life for the coming decade, causing the GPS evangelism strategies to fall apart.

When new leadership was installed at NAMB and began responding to the GCR recommendations, the team that put together *God's Plan for Sharing* was summarily dismantled and the budget and personnel for evangelism were reallocated. A decade has passed since the approval of the GCR proposals, but the infrastructure, the energy, and the attention of SBC churches on reaching their communities with the Gospel has still not recovered from the internal chaos unleashed by the GCR proposals. Today's NAMB is probably incapable of putting together a national evangelism initiative on that scale. Muscles in the body that atrophy from lack of use take a long time to restore. The evangelism muscles

Today's NAMB is probably incapable of putting together a national evangelism initiative on that scale.

that were long at the core of the Southern Baptist identity have atrophied over the last ten years and will take years to restore and rebuild, even if the will to do so returns to Southern Baptist life. As for the benefits of replacing the emphasis on evangelism with an emphasis on church planting, the 2013 goal of starting 1,500 churches a year has been replaced by a new goal of starting 600 new churches a year, a reduction of more than 50%. Today NAMB refuses to report how many of its appointed missionaries are assigned to some aspect of church planting. Withholding such basic information from the Convention is rarely a sign of good news, especially when the budget for church planting is now in excess of $70,000,000. With massive dollars readily at hand, NAMB can't find enough church planters or start enough churches to keep up with population growth and annual loss of churches. Having money but not enough missionaries is a very unusual problem for Southern Baptists.

The evangelism muscles that were long at the core of the Southern Baptist identity have atrophied over the last ten years and will take years to restore and rebuild, even if the will to do so returns to Southern Baptist life.

Charles S. Kelley Jr.

The failure of the GCR task force to incorporate, recommend, or even mention a new, carefully planned, widely supported initiative to share the Gospel with every person in the nation and call them to repentance and faith in Christ is one of the greatest miscalculations in the history of the Southern Baptist Convention. The negative impact of that miscalculation was exacerbated by the GCR-inspired decision of the new NAMB leadership to turn away from its historic role in Southern Baptist evangelism and replace it with hyper attention to church planting. Neither church planting nor evangelism thrived after this reordering of priorities. Instead of using the gift of a carefully planned opportunity to keep fanning the flame of Great Commission engagement across the SBC for at least a decade into the future, GCR became a "one and done" presidential initiative that quickly faded away from SBC conversations and took *God's Plan for Sharing* with it. Unintentionally that oversight opened the door for a decade of unprecedented statistical decline. As a result of this massive miscalculation, a decade further down the road Southern Baptists find themselves still without a fresh understanding of their Great Commission identity and mission as the future unfolds. Treading water can keep you afloat, but it does not get you anywhere. Southern Baptists know they want to reach the world, but they are still waiting for a clear, inspiring strategy on how to do it. The GCR

Task Force ignored the obvious opportunity of *God's Plan for Sharing*, a steadily escalating emphasis on the Great Commission at every level of SBC life for the coming decade and the

Treading water can keep you afloat, but it does not get you anywhere. Southern Baptists know they want to reach the world, but they are still waiting for a clear, inspiring strategy on how to do it.

SBC continues to pay the price for being oblivious to the obvious.

LESSON FOUR:
THE ESSENCE OF WARFARE IS LOGISTICS

Most books on military history include some version of this simple sentence: "The essence of warfare is logistics." When asked about the accuracy of that statement, the second in command at a US military base told this writer: "Around here we say amateurs plan strategy, but professionals plan logistics." Merriam Webster dictionary defines logistics as "the handling of the details of an operation." An army needs soldiers to fight a war, but military leaders also know that if you cannot feed those soldiers, you cannot fight them. Any decision to deploy more personnel in the field requires a decision to increase the logistical support necessary for effectiveness in the field. An arrowhead is not nearly as effective a weapon without the whole arrow and a bow behind it. The International Mission Board became a textbook illustration of this reality. After years of lamenting having more missionary candidates than funding for needed positions, the IMB pulled out all the stops and used every possible dollar to expand rapidly the number of missionaries in the field. Eventually, however, the Board realized they had appointed an unsustainable number of missionaries. Paying the salaries of a higher number of missionaries without adequate funding for the logistical support those missionaries needed was unsustainable. The whole SBC was shocked when missionaries were brought home and asked to retire or otherwise move on because the IMB could not afford the missionary force it already had. Inevitably the number of missionaries had to be in sync with the necessary logistical support. Logistics play a crucial role in the success of a mission. To think that the only thing necessary to enlarge Great Commission impact is to increase the number of missionaries in the field is a most naïve perspective.

The Southern Baptist Convention can be described as a collection of fully autonomous units (churches, conventions, entities, etc.) acting in voluntary, continuous cooperation. There is no single logistical pipeline supporting all SBC churches in their ministry efforts. Each church is responsible for raising and spending its own budget in light of its own capacities. But the founding of the SBC created opportunities for likeminded churches to work together to do things no single church could do, such as missions and theological education. Toward that end the creation of the Cooperative Program and the two offerings for International and North American missions enabled Southern Baptists to provide a network of logistical support for Convention ministries outside of a local church in a given area or region, from countywide to worldwide. The desire to cooperate with other churches in order to do big and important things was matched with a means for those cooperative ministries to be funded in a sustainable way.

As the Cooperative Program grew and provided a stable source of funding for the necessary logistical support of ministries outside of any one local church, something very important happened. The entities and ministries supported by CP began feeding logistical support back into the local churches of the SBC, helping them accomplish their work in reaching their communities for Christ. This was especially true of the Home Mission Board/ North American Mission Board. Other denominations and non-Baptist churches were often envious of the great variety of resources and logistical support available to the Convention's churches. Many of the existing churches that one day choose to be-come Southern Baptist churches are drawn by the resources that become available to them as an SBC church. This network of logistical support blos-somed in new ways after the emergence of the Co-operative Agreements in the mid-twentieth century. The Cooperative Agreements left the SBC principle of the autonomy of churches, conventions, and en-tities firmly in place, but it significantly improved the clarity of communication and coordination and made reduplication of efforts much less common. CP funds given by all SBC churches were providing some means of logistical support for all SBC church-es through the associational and state convention networks as well as funding the missionary and theological education initiatives of the Convention. In addition to initiatives for evangelism, church planting, and social needs ministry, NAMB also in-cluded funding for administrative support, pastoral support, and leadership development. Such sup-port was vital to creating a supportive network for churches planted in states with little or no Baptist presence. Also important was the time NAMB per-sonnel spent in the field conducting training events, leadership development, and strategic planning for churches, associations, and state conventions. With that network of logistical support funneled through these strategic partnerships between HMB/NAMB and state conventions and associations, the SBC experienced explosive growth and became a national body extending far beyond its Southern roots.

The Convention spotlight typically shines on evangelism and church planting initiatives, but it was the lower profile logistical support out of the spotlight that significantly undergirded SBC expansion. Because the promotion and collection of funds for the Cooperative Program was assigned to the state conventions, the task of making existing state conventions stronger and creating new state conventions and associations as the SBC moved into new territory was critical for the health of CP. The Convention reorganization that came with the Covenant for a New Century initiative in 1995 attempted to reassign more responsibility for CP promotion and stewardship promotion to the Executive Committee. However, the GCR task force recognized that change did not unfold as expected and recommended primary CP promotion and stewardship promotion go back to the state conventions. The region by region, state conventions were closer to the great mass of SBC churches than the Executive Committee, a national entity, could ever be. In the words of the task force:

> The reason for this is straightforward and easy to see. The state conventions have the mechanism in place to collect funds and promote the Cooperative Program. This has been their his-

toric role and continuing passion (*2010 SBC Annual*, p. 86).

Logistics at the local level are crucial to achieving desired outcomes at the national and international levels. As the IMB example mentioned above illustrates, the health of local SBC churches will inevitably affect the health of the SBC mission enterprise no matter how many missionaries are on the field. The IMB attempted to expand its missionary count while SBC churches were in decline. Logistical support could not keep up with the expansion, and missionaries already deployed on the field experienced the consequences. Planning to increase the number of missionaries without also planning to increase the logistical support behind and around them is planning to eventually fail.

The logistics factor was largely ignored by the GCR task force. It was especially ignored in the response of NAMB to GCR recommendations. Large numbers of staff were eliminated and travel to lead conferences and training events and engage in strategic planning with state conventions and associations was dramatically reduced. Funds for administrative and other forms of logistical support in state conventions and associations were curtailed or eliminated.

If the goal of pulling money out of state conventions and associations and reducing the engagement of NAMB personnel in field support and training for pastors and church leaders was to be able to hire and deploy more missionaries to the field, that decision backfired. Both the IMB and NAMB have fewer missionaries than pre-GCR days. The number of new church starts is down nearly 50%, and NAMB regularly says it cannot find enough qualified candidates to serve as church planters. The typical SBC church has become less healthy, the churches in a geographic area have become less connected to each other, and the missionary enterprise of the SBC experienced a negative impact. Southern Baptists are becoming another illustration of the essential role of logistics for the church militant and not just for a nation's military. At this point in the SBC story, one could argue that Convention data indicates the need for

If the goal of pulling money out of state conventions and associations and reducing the engagement of NAMB personnel in field support and training for pastors and church leaders was to be able to hire and deploy more missionaries to the field, that decision backfired. Both the IMB and NAMB have fewer missionaries than pre-GCR days. The number of new church starts is down nearly 50%, and NAMB regularly says it cannot find enough qualified candidates to serve as church planters.

better logistical support for the churches and missionaries we have is more important to the future than increasing the number of missionaries on the field. Sustained growth is more likely

The typical SBC church has become less healthy, the churches in a geographic area have become less connected to each other, and the missionary enterprise of the SBC experienced a negative impact.

to come from healthy churches than logistical budget cuts. A critical question for the future of the SBC is: How can SBC entities, the state conventions, and local associations work together to both strengthen local churches and harness their energy and resources to fulfill the Great Commission?

LESSON FIVE:
EVALUATING THE EFFECTS OF CHANGE IS IMPERATIVE

In many Baptist circles, most attempts to change rarely receive a warm welcome. People who are comfortable with the way things are often find doing things differently to be an uncomfortable experience. One should be careful not to evaluate change too quickly. Change always comes with negative perceptions because it tends to unsettle the settled. But, there is one thing worse than evaluating any major change too quickly. That one thing worse is being so invested in implementing major change that one fails to evaluate honestly its effect. For the best possible future, the Southern Baptist Convention must develop the habit of assessing what happened after it approves major initiatives. In the case of the subject of this assessment, the SBC has not experienced a Great Commission Resurgence by any standard of measure in the ten years since the GCR recommendations were approved and acted upon. Nearly all meaningful statistical categories used to measure SBC progress are down significantly. As indicated in the charts included herein, the decade since GCR was approved is the worst statistical decade in SBC history. There is no need to be angry with anyone, and any attempt to assign blame for a major initiative that did not deliver as promised is pointless. What does matter is an evaluation of outcomes from new initiatives and conversations about what should follow those evaluations. In

One should be careful not to evaluate change too quickly. Change always comes with negative perceptions because it tends to unsettle the settled. But, there is one thing worse than evaluating any major change too quickly. That one thing worse is being so invested in implementing major change that one fails to evaluate honestly its effect.

the case of GCR, the question of where we go from here must be addressed. If a Great Commission Resurgence was needed then, it is surely needed now.

As indicated in the charts included herein, the decade since GCR was approved is the worst statistical decade in SBC history.

Some of the GCR proposals proved to be inconsequential and as such are not worth further attention. The missional statement and values statement had zero effect on the SBC. They are doing no harm. Let them be. The concept of Great Commission Giving generated enormous controversy at the time of the GCR proposals, dominating nearly all GCR discussions. After a decade it has largely faded into the background noise of the SBC. There is likely a trickle effect draining some support for the Cooperative Program, but addressing it further in any way seems unlikely to have potential benefit for Southern Baptists. After ten years of diminishing impact, there is little to gain in the further promotion of Great Commission Giving and less to gain by attempting to undo it. As background noise it carries little potential good or harm. Unless the SBC decides to make radical changes in the Cooperative Program, staying in the little noticed background noise of the Convention seems to be the best future for Great Commission Giving. It is an experiment that never gained traction as either a badge of honor for designated givers or a reliable statistical indicator of significance for understanding much about the state of giving in the SBC. It certainly did not help or strengthen CP, but what is done is done. What is necessary is the revitalization of the Cooperative Program. An opportunity was missed to help the rising generation of Southern Baptists fall in love with and be energized about CP. The future of the Cooperative Program needs massive attention.

The most shocking statistic the writer found in this study was the record of how many SBC churches did not give a dime to CP, a number that appears to have climbed significantly higher since GCR. As noted above, the source of that pre-COVID data was the *SBC Life Journal, Summer* 2021, a publication of the SBC Executive Committee. No other financial plan by a family of churches in American history has generated more money for missions and ministry than the CP strategy did for Southern Baptists. Is the Convention going to stay the course with CP into the future? If so, it absolutely must capture afresh the imagination of the rising generation of Southern Baptists. By the standards of measure used by the SBC for decades, the decline of Cooperative Program support in SBC churches is a reality. For churches to feel connected to and invested in the SBC, multiple connecting points between churches are needed. Many of those traditional connecting points have been frayed and weakened in the last decade, and those weakened relationships are showing up most vividly in declining CP support. It is an issue needing aggressive attention and the intentional repair of relationships between the state conventions, NAMB, and the SBC. This is a red flag warning.

The most significant GCR changes that must be evaluated by Southern Baptists are the changes that have happened at the North American Mission Board. Apparently the GCR Task Force wanted dramatic change at NAMB, and they got it. The Cooperative Agreements that played a large role in driving the explosive growth of the SBC into all fifty states and its status as the largest denomination in America were eliminated. The regionally-based national strategy for evangelism and church planting reflecting the voluntary partnerships of autonomous orga-

For churches to feel connected to and invested in the SBC, multiple connecting points between churches are needed. Many of those traditional connecting points have been frayed and weakened in the last decade, and those weakened relationships are showing up most vividly in declining CP support. It is an issue needing aggressive attention and the intentional repair of relationships between the state conventions, NAMB, and the SBC. This is a red flag warning.

nizations was replaced by a corporate approach to strategy based on centralized planning and control fueled by a very different way of using the cash given to NAMB through CP and the Annie Armstrong Offering. Requiring state convention executives to sign Non-Disclosure Agreements if their conventions receive funds from NAMB is a very different kind of Cooperative Agreement, one that signals nothing about partnership and much about control.

The profound shift away from evangelism in order to magnify church planting was the other dramatic change at NAMB. By vote of SBC messengers in 1906 and again in the Covenant for a New Century reorganization that transformed the Home Mission Board into the NAMB of today, the responsibility to promote evangelism across the SBC and develop evangelism strategies and resources for churches to use to reach the lost in their communities was specifically assigned to the North American Mission Board. As already described and documented, evangelism at NAMB is a shadow of what it was pre-GCR. A decade of statistics from SBC churches are now in hand after this change. Measure the statistics against any other decade in SBC history and the reality of an evangelism crisis is clear, with little indication of positive improvement to come.

To repeat one example: In 1939 the SBC had 25,018 churches and 4,949,174 members. 2,010 of those churches owned no facilities. In spite of all

As described and documented above, evangelism at NAMB is a shadow of what it was pre-GCR. A decade of statistics from SBC churches are now in hand after this change. Measure the statistics against any other decade in SBC history and the reality of an evangelism crisis is clear, with little indication of positive improvement to come.

the struggles associated with coming out of the Great Depression, SBC churches baptized 269,155 people. In 2019, prior to the COVID pandemic, the SBC had 47,530 churches and 14,525,579 members, but those churches only baptized 235,748 people (33,407 fewer than SBC churches in 1939). The ten years prior to the GCR-inspired changes at NAMB saw a net increase of 4,139 SBC churches added to the SBC after spending a total of $227,448,246 on church planting during the decade. The decade after the GCR-inspired strategy saw a net increase in SBC churches of only1,887 additional churches after spending a total of $667,391,815 on church planting. In the history of the SBC there has never been that kind of gap in the net total of SBC churches and budget funds for church planting in a comparison of NAMB's impact on the SBC in back-to-back decades. The strategic plan of NAMB for the last decade and a comprehensive examination of the outcomes it produced in SBC churches must be carefully evaluated. This is a red flag warning.

The questions facing the Southern Baptist Convention and its churches one decade after the Great Commission Resurgence proposals were adopted include two simple questions. We cannot be distracted by the pointless question of whether or not the GCR process was necessary or whether or not it was handled

The strategic plan of NAMB for the last decade and a comprehensive examination of the outcomes it produced in SBC churches must be carefully evaluated. This is a red flag warning.

appropriately. It happened and it did affect the SBC. We must acknowledge without reservation or hesitation that those involved in the GCR process and in implementing the GCR recommendations were all people who love Jesus, who have effective ministries and who were doing their best to serve Him and the churches of the SBC. We cannot waste time on whether or not those involved who did not have the benefit of the hindsight revealed in the passing of a decade should be criticized or blamed for their good faith efforts. The answer is no. Again, no one did anything but his best to serve Jesus and His people called Southern Baptists. Undoing the past is not an option. Understanding the present and anticipating the future are the critical points of focus. There are times in the life of any organization, including the SBC, when trying new things

We must acknowledge without reservation or hesitation that those involved in the GCR process and in implementing the GCR recommendations were all people who love Jesus, who have effective ministries and who were doing their best to serve Him and the churches of the SBC. We cannot waste time on whether or not those involved who did not have the benefit of the hindsight revealed in the passing of a decade should be criticized or blamed for their good faith efforts.

or doing things differently seems to be the best path forward into the future. But implementing major change carries with it a responsibility to evaluate the effects the change produced after a reasonable time has passed. I am sure there are those who would disagree with all or part of this assessment. However, I hope all will think carefully about two simple, unavoidable questions this writer feels grew out of this project.

The first of those simple questions is this: Are Southern Baptists going to continue to rely upon the Cooperative Program as the central channel, the lifeblood of funding for SBC ministries? If the answer is yes, immediate and thorough attention from all stakeholders must be given to explore ways to refresh and excite Southern Baptists and their churches about the value and power of this extraordinary approach to fundraising. If the answer is no, serious

Are Southern Baptists going to continue to rely upon the Cooperative Program as the central channel, the lifeblood of funding for SBC ministries?

conversation about a replacement for the role of the Cooperative Program in funding SBC ministries must begin immediately. If present trends continue, CP faces serious challenges to its future viability. This writer votes for refreshing CP.

The second of those simple questions is this: Has the time come for the North American Mission Board to make significant adjustments to the post-GCR strategy it implemented? The International Mission Board and the North American Mission Board are the ties that bind Southern Baptists and their churches together. The GCR Task Force gave relatively little attention to the IMB, and recommended tweaks, not major changes. Those tweaks did not upset any apple carts, although the decline of SBC giving to CP did create a major fiscal crisis that resulted in missionaries being brought home. Few if any attributed that to GCR. NAMB was at the heart of the GCR proposals. The impact of the resulting

Has the time come for the North American Mission Board to make significant adjustments to the post-GCR strategy it implemented?

strategy of NAMB, however, was entirely different. Tensions with the state conventions reached an unthinkable level and are affecting the very fabric of SBC connections and in all likelihood, the health of the Cooperative Program. The turning away from evangelism appears to be a major factor in the biggest evangelism crisis in SBC history. In spite of a huge shift of funding and attention to church planting, NAMB was unable to reach its own church planting goals. In 2013 the SBC was told the Convention needed to start 1,500 new churches each year in order to keep up with population growth and the loss of churches over time. In 2021 only 600 new church plants were recorded. NAMB has twice lowered its goal from 1,500 new church plants, seeking a target it will be able to hit. NAMB has provided an illustration for the ages that evangelism and church planting are related, but they are not identical. Are Southern Baptists satisfied with the Great Commission progress of SBC churches in North America during the last decade, or is it time to make some adjustments to a strategy that has been largely unchanged during the post-GCR decade? This writer votes for adjusting the strategy.

NAMB has provided an illustration for the ages that evangelism and church planting are related, but they are not identical.

The Last Word

The purpose of this assessment is twofold. First, to identify and evaluate what actually happened in the SBC after the 2010 SBC messengers approved the recommendations from the Great Commission Task Force. Each component of the GCR proposal was identified and the actions taken after the Convention described. The descriptions are followed by a look at what actually happened. One result is a comprehensive report of SBC data collected year by year for a decade in the easy to read format of charts. I have not found a comparable collection of these basic points of SBC data over the course of at least a decade in any other public source. The content and evaluation included in this assessment reflect my perspective on that data as I have sought to understand at least some of the ways the SBC was affected by the Great Commission Resurgence.

The second purpose is to stimulate conversation among Southern Baptists about the present and future of this beloved Convention. The SBC faces a crossroad moment. How Southern Baptists respond to the circumstances of this moment will define the future that unfolds. The survival of the Southern Baptist Convention is not in question, but its viability as a family of churches in the vanguard of God's Great Commission agenda is less certain. I describe myself as an Optimistic Pessimist. I know how serious and precarious a position we are in at this moment. But I also know that God is able to empower His people for His purposes in any circumstance. The question is: Will He? More to the point, Are Southern Baptists going to be a people God wants to empower for His purposes? The answers to those questions have never been less certain than they are today. In light of that conviction, let's talk to each other. Let's not waste time looking for heroes or villains. Let's not vent anger or frustration with each other. Let's not focus on exuberance about what we love in the SBC or discouragement about what disappoints us. Let's accept what the data reveals: We are a Convention clearly in decline. Now, where do we go from here?. At this point, the great American inventor Thomas Alva Edison would probably offer something like this advice to us: "Congratulations. You have found some things that did not work as expected. Now get back to work! Stay at it until you do find the things that produce the results you seek." That is the point of this assessment.

> *The survival of the Southern Baptist Convention is not in question, but its viability as a family of churches in the vanguard of God's Great Commission agenda is less certain.*

Chuck Kelley
Fairhope, AL

AFTERWORD

By Junior Hill

Chuck Kelley and I share more than a passion for evangelism. The parents of his wife Rhonda, Joyce and Bob Harrington, lived next door to Carole and me when we were students at New Orleans Baptist Seminary. When Rhonda Harrington married this young evangelist Chuck Kelley, we paid attention. It turned out that he was a passionate advocate for evangelism, and our friendship put down some deep roots!

Any Southern Baptist who knows my friend Chuck Kelley is aware that he has been a diligent student and a keen observer of Southern Baptist evangelism. Twenty-five years ago he warned Southern Baptists that they were "a harvest-oriented denomination living in the midst of an unseeded generation." This country boy took that as a serious warning. After a careful analysis of the state of evangelism in the SBC covering the last ten years,

Brother Chuck issued an even more serious warning: Southern Baptists are on the verge of losing their interest in the harvest, largely ignoring what has (and has not been happening) in our churches.

The biggest evangelism crisis is within our Convention and churches. Every Southern Baptist–pastors and leaders in the churches as well as those sitting on the pews–would be wise to read, to think about, and to talk about the carefully documented things happening in the SBC and its churches during the decade since the Great Commission Resurgence was introduced. In light of this steady decline in evangelism and church planting, we must all have as our primary goal telling people about Jesus and calling upon them to turn to Christ and be saved. We will do it best if we can all do it together and not be distracted from the main thing. Let's just do it! We must move ahead of the problem, searching and inquiring about how to meet the need for compelling evangelism. We need to think about it, talk about it, and get the SBC back to doing what Southern Baptists have always done–tell lost people about Jesus and urge them to say yes to Him.

Junior Hill
Evangelist
Hartselle, Alabama

A PERSONAL TESTIMONY
from
Mark Coppenger

I was raised in the Southern Baptist church, benefiting from a range of programs and emphases, but when I answered a call to prepare for the pastorate, I was intimidated by the prospects. I'd been a philosophy prof for seven years, and when I got to seminary, I found myself "drinking from a firehose" as I tried to get up to speed on sermon preparation, Greek and Hebrew, church music, etc.

Thankful to say, Southern Baptists didn't drop me with a "good luck" after graduation. I was soon gratified and even astonished at the array of denominational programs and resources available to me over the next several decades–from the Sunday School Board (MasterLife); the Foreign Mission Board (a state partnership with Brazil); and the Home Mission Board (as I served in the local church, association, state convention, and seminary) with Continuing Witness Training; Prayer for Spiritual Awakening; Crossover; Mission Service Corps; Interfaith Witness; Cooperative Agreements, funding evangelism conferences, church plants, and state staff; the Nehemiah Project; "Here's Hope" Simultaneous Revivals; Strategic-Focus Cities; and the One-Day Soul-Winning Workshop. Along the way, at the Executive Committee, I got to tell the story of how this whole, wonderful web of congregational and denominational entities worked together to do great things, including four church-starts a day.

Yes, there were tensions, blunders, slackers, and us knuckleheads in the life and work of our big, messy denomination. But God blessed our mess. And then we got "smarter and smarter" as we streamlined and centralized our approaches, but, somehow, we seem to have outsmarted ourselves. As Dr. Kelley demonstrates, there has been a precipitous drop in baptisms, church plants, and Cooperative Program support.

Yes, of course, there have been a number of factors, some of which he lists. I'd add that we've also been damaged internally by misbehavior in some of our agencies, whether in the form of social "ingratiationism" (wokeness, obsession with winsomeness, and craven concern with PR) or the powerplays of executive worldliness.

The language of the "Great Commission Resurgence" was noble and well-intended, but "the road to disintegration can be paved with good intentions." And I thank Dr. Kelley for so aptly demonstrating this.

Mark Coppenger, PhD

Appendix I

Correspondence Between State Convention Executives, the North American Mission Board, and the SBC Executive Committee

The Best Intentions

To: *Dr. Kevin Ezell, President of the North American Mission Board and NAMB Trustees*
       Dr. Ronnie Floyd, President of the SBC Executive Committee and SBC Executive
       Committee

This letter is being sent to the leadership of the North American Mission Board (NAMB) and the Executive Committee of the Southern Baptist Convention on behalf of the undersigned Baptist state convention leaders in response to the "Strategic Cooperation Agreements" sent by NAMB to non-South Baptist state conventions, dated June 26-30, 2020.

Our state conventions have appreciated our respective partnerships over the years with the North American Mission Board, especially in the areas of church planting and evangelism, and also in coordinated missions and mobilization efforts such as disaster relief. We believe we work most effectively when working in collaboration and harmony, especially in our non-South states where the local context and cultures of our mission fields can vary so significantly.

Over the past ten years, NAMB has grown increasingly centralized and unilaterally directive in its strategies, its personnel and funding processes, and its relationships with state conventions. While this has not been our desire, and we are convinced the results reveal diminished fruitfulness, we have respected NAMB's autonomy. Our state conventions have made many adjustments to cooperate with NAMB's evolving and frequently changing strategies and guidelines. Some state conventions believe NAMB hasn't kept previous agreements. In spite of this, we have greatly reduced staff and state-directed ministry to provide Cooperative Program funds to the national SBC.

However, we find that the latest, revised "Strategic Cooperation Agreement" for October, 2020-September, 2023 abandons true collaborative partnership. For one thing, it leaves state conventions with little or no role in the assessment, supervision, or evaluation of church planters or statewide personnel. In addition, though NAMB notified state conventions on August 7 and conceded to fund evangelism for one more year in the same manner that was planned for 2020 (evangelism funding through state conventions has been frozen since mid-March), moving forward we have little confidence with which to plan for evangelism funding from NAMB in our annual operating budgets, and we have been told that undesignated "administrative funding" would be reduced by half in 2021 and then eliminated in the years following. This means that NAMB will provide no certain funding through non-south state conventions beginning in 2022. Tens of millions of dollars that were once part of funding church planting and evangelism through non-south state conventions is now part of NAMB's budget, directed exclusively by NAMB, for work in our states.

An agreement that reflects little collaborative partnership and that promises much reduced investment in state strategies, offers little value to our state conventions. As a result of these and other concerns, many of us feel the proposed agreements are simply not in our best interest. Indeed, after years of attrition, many of us believe our longstanding partnerships with NAMB may finally be coming to an end in any meaningful sense.

As we have attempted to understand how we fit into the evolving NAMB paradigm and continue to support the work of the churches in our state conventions, many of us and our boards

206

ave contemplated such responses as declining to enter into any agreements with NAMB, retaining a larger percentage of Cooperative Program funds for the work of the state conventions, designating giving only to specific SBC work, reducing promotion of the Annie Armstrong Easter Offering and replacing it with a more robust state missions offering, or even creating unique state-facilitated partnerships. Some of us would like to go on an annual block-grant system like southern state conventions. They each receive $300,000 annually from NAMB. No non-south convention will receive even close to this amount by October 2021. These options, as well as others that have been discussed, are not what we prefer, but NAMB's reduction in funding through State Conventions totals over $50 million annually, and we must be ready to do what is necessary to support the ongoing work of the churches in our home states who look to us for contextualized assistance in church planting, evangelism, and missions.

Please understand the issue prompting us to respond is partnership. Our concern is with the way NAMB dictates the terms of the relationship between various state conventions. This most current "cooperation agreement," like others before it, included no discussion with the leadership of our respective conventions as to what would be most effective in our states. We were simply informed as to how it will be. God will provide the resources we need one way or another, but we would rather be in partnership with NAMB working together to reach the lost and make disciples than each going our own way. We remain committed to the shared goals of Southern Baptists that are so beautifully illustrated by the Cooperative Program. It is the desire of every state convention executive director signing this letter to be net contributors to missions through the Cooperative Program and our shared causes. In recent years non-south conventions have given about $46 million annually through the national SBC when all giving channels are combined.

We are reaching out to you now to try to avoid any escalation that will become more and more public, with additional boards and leaders in our states getting involved. Dr. Leo Endel is serving as the president of our Baptist State Conventions Executive Director group for 2020-21 and Dr. Sonny Tucker is our president elect for 2021-22. For simplicity and clarity of communication, we propose that you direct any response to Dr. Endel for his coordination with the undersigned. Of course you may also feel free to respond directly to all of us simultaneously if you choose. We respectfully ask for a response prior to August 15. We are praying for you as you consider our concerns.

Sincerely,

Randy Adams
Signature

Northwest Baptist Convention

State Convention

Randy Adams
Printed Name

The Best Intentions

Bill Agee

_____

Signature

California Southern Baptist Convention

_____

State Convention

Christopher Martin

_____

Signature

Hawaii Pacific Baptist Convention

_____

State Convention

Jack Kwok

_____

Signature

State Convention of Baptists in Ohio

_____

State Convention

Joseph Bunce

_____

Signature

Baptist Convention Of New Mexico

_____

State Convention

Randy Covington

_____

Signature

Alaska Baptist Resource Network

_____

State Convention

Bill Agee	
Printed Name	
Christopher Martin	
Printed Name	
Jack Kwok	
Printed Name	
Joseph Bunce	
Printed Name	
Randy Covington	
Printed Name	

Charles S. Kelley Jr.

North American Mission Board

4200 North Point Pkwy. Alpharetta, GA 30022
770.410.6000 | 800.634.2462 | NAMB.NET

August 17, 2020

Randy Adams, Northwest Baptist Convention
Bill Agee, California Southern Baptist Convention
Joseph Bunce, New Mexico Baptist Convention
Randy Convington, Alaska Baptist Resource Network
Jack Kwok, State Convention of Baptists in Ohio
Chris Martin, Hawaii Pacific Baptist Convention

Gentlemen:

We received your August 12 letter addressed to Kevin Ezell, Dr. Floyd, the SBC Executive Committee, and our NAMB Board of Trustees. As an autonomous Southern Baptist entity, it is most appropriate for a response to come from us.

The NAMB Board of Trustees wholeheartedly supports President Ezell and our staff in the direction NAMB is taking in fulfilling our ministry assignments with churches, associations, and state conventions.

You have correctly identified that we are more focused (centralized) and directive in our strategies, personnel and funding. We're not sure you could make a more complimentary accusation of us! NAMB trustees expect our leaders to develop and implement strategies that accomplish our ministry assignments and to then fund those strategies specifically.

We take very seriously the task of being good stewards of the funds given to NAMB by SBC churches through the Cooperative Program and the Annie Armstrong Easter Offering. We certainly do and will continue to assess and evaluate all the planters and all the personnel we fund. We have no intention of delegating these responsibilities to any ministry partner.

This is not a lack of cooperation or partnership; it is our way of stewarding the resources we invest in NAMB strategies. Many ministry partners, including our three churches, have found this to be incredibly helpful and effective in identifying and retaining the best candidates for the important roles that NAMB is funding. We believe if you will give it a chance you will find the same to be true.

You stated that we had no discussions with state conventions, but this is simply not true. In March of this year, Kevin and our board vice chairman, Eric Thomas, traveled to

The Best Intentions

Oregon to meet with the leadership of the Northwest Baptist Convention to do just that. Our leadership is always willing and open to meet and discuss ways we can better serve Southern Baptists together.

We look forward to hearing your ideas and to our future conversations as together we pursue the goal of taking the Gospel to every corner of North America and beyond.

Your Brothers in Christ,

Danny de Armas
Chairman
NAMB Board of Trustees

Eric J. Thomas
Vice Chairman

William L. Rice
Second Vice Chairman

Charles S. Kelley Jr.

COOPERATION IS THE WAY FORWARD

In August 2020, the Southern Baptist Convention Executive Committee and the North American Mission Board (NAMB) received a letter of request from six Baptist state convention leaders who were concerned about the Strategic Partnership Agreements sent to them by NAMB. Their appeal to the SBC Executive Committee was to intervene for the sake of partnership, collaboration, and cooperation with NAMB.

According to SBC Bylaw 18.E(5), the SBC Executive Committee is, "To act in an **advisory** capacity on all questions of cooperation among the different entities of the Convention, and among the entities of the Convention and those of other conventions, whether state or national." Understanding this responsibility, the SBC Executive Committee Officers and Executive Leadership Team felt the need to respond to this appeal regarding matters of cooperation between state conventions and NAMB.

This resulted in the SBC Executive Committee Officers and Executive Leadership Team meeting with the six state convention leaders who were accompanied by six additional state convention leaders. All of these represented non-south Baptist bodies.

At a later date, a similar meeting occurred with Dr. Kevin Ezell, NAMB President, one of his staff members, and three key NAMB trustee officers. SBC Bylaw 18.E(9) instructs the Executive Committee "to maintain open channels of communication between the Executive Committee and the trustees of the entities of the Convention, to study and make recommendations to entities concerning adjustments required by ministry statements or by established Convention policies and practices,". We are grateful for the helpful engagement of these NAMB trustees.

In both of these extensive meetings, the SBC Executive Committee Officers and Executive Leadership Team listened intently to both groups. We are grateful the non-south state executive directors and NAMB leaders were very open and clear in sharing their experiences and the details of their situations.

During this process, each time the SBC Executive Committee Officers met, these matters were discussed as we searched for ways we could advise these Baptist bodies to have a renewal in their cooperation. Additional meetings and conversations occurred with other state convention leaders. The purpose was to seek counsel on how to move forward through this challenge. The input and wisdom of these state convention leaders have been important in this process.

The SBC Executive Committee has completed our role with respect to this request from the six state conventions, and we issue our advice toward cooperation to all parties involved in these matters. With humility, we submit these advisements to you.

1. It is very important that each of us remember Jesus desires for us to walk in unity together. Jesus' prayer recorded in John 17:21, "May they all be one, as you, Father are in me and I am in you. May they also be in us, so that the world may believe you sent me." We appeal to all parties to walk in unity together as a testimony to the world.

The Best Intentions

2. Our Great Commission work is dependent on our cooperation. Article 14 of *The Baptist Faith and Message* clearly reminds us of this united confession of cooperation. Indeed, cooperation is the way forward. Our cooperation will never be any greater than our relationships. Relationships and cooperation are built through effective, constant communication. Cooperative relationships demand a commitment to communicating honestly, clearly, and consistently.

   According to the SBC Organization Manual and NAMB's approved mission statement, the SBC has instructed NAMB "to work with churches, associations and state conventions in mobilizing Southern Baptists as a missional force to impact North America with the Gospel of Jesus Christ through evangelism and church planting." Cooperation is the only way forward to mobilize all Southern Baptists as a missional force to impact North America with the Gospel of Jesus Christ through evangelism and church planting.

   Southern Baptists are deeply concerned for the overwhelming lostness that clearly exists across the non-south regions of North America. In response, we encourage NAMB to find every way possible to push more resources into these areas through increases in financial resources, missionaries, evangelism strategies, and more strategic partnerships and platforms with every Southern Baptist body and with Southern Baptist churches in these areas. We appreciate NAMB for allocating resources linked to collaborative strategies in order to penetrate lostness. The SBC also strongly desires for associations and state conventions to cooperate with NAMB in these efforts. We affirm that each state convention is unique with its own needs and opportunities, and therefore, a "one size fits all" approach is inadequate. We encourage each state convention to meet with NAMB to develop a path for your future partnership together. Each state convention has value; therefore, please do all you can to allocate resources through the Cooperative Program as we work together to advance the gospel across the entire globe. Cooperation is the Baptist way; therefore, each of us needs to renew our efforts to cooperate together through communication, collaboration, and relationships to reach North America for Christ. The desperate needs of lost people and the call of the Gospel demand this of us all.

3. The greatest resource our Southern Baptist family has is one another. We are thankful for how many state conventions in the South have partnerships with non-south state conventions. Therefore, we encourage the leaders of all our state conventions to work in cooperation with one another and with NAMB to advance the gospel to places and people groups where the gospel is needed. This kind of willingness, assistance, and cooperation demonstrates the strength of everyone working together for the cause of Christ today and serves as a good example of cooperation for the future.

4. Since the SBC Executive Committee has begun meeting with these entities, NAMB has reestablished an ongoing schedule of meetings with non-south conventions to establish a path forward for the future. We are thankful for the willingness of these state conventions and NAMB to continue working toward cooperation in this manner. It is

vital to the testimony of our efforts to mobilize our churches to work together that we all be mutually accountable in these renewed efforts to cooperate together. We will continue to pray for and affirm these meetings.

Through the years, Southern Baptists have demonstrated a great desire to advance the Gospel across North America. Our cooperation has led to planting thousands of churches in North America and enabling us to minister to the thousands of existing churches. Cooperation is our path forward.

Finally, for the sake of reaching lost people and advancing the Gospel to all of North America and across the entire world, we call upon our churches, our state conventions, and our national entities to a renewed cooperation so we can give Good News to the whole world.

One of the best examples of cooperation within the SBC is the Cooperative Program. We affirm the Cooperative Program is the most efficient, effective system for funding the ministries of state conventions and the Southern Baptist Convention. Our cooperation together in reaching the lost leads our churches to cooperation with us through the Cooperative Program. This is why we must do all that we can to prioritize, elevate, and accelerate our giving through the Cooperative Program.

The Cooperative Program is the financial fuel to reach every person for Jesus Christ in every town, every city, every state, and every nation. We must all reaffirm our commitment to work together, collaborate together, cooperate together, and pray together. This is why we believe cooperation is the way forward.

Appendix II
SBC Data Charts

Decadal Percentage Changes
in SBC Giving (1870–2021) —————————— 216

SBC Missions (2010–2021) ————————— 216

SBC Giving Trends (2012–2021) —————— 218

Annual Great Commission Giving (2011–2021) — 219

The SBC After GCR (2010–2021) ——————— 220

Non-CP Churches in the SBC (2010–2021) ——— 222

Church Planting Before GCR (2000–2010) ——— 222

Church Planting After GCR (2011–2021) ——— 223

Decadal Percentage Changes in SBC Giving (1970-2021)

Years	Total Receipts in SBC Churches	Total of Undes-ignated Gifts to SBC Churches	Total CP Gifts from SBC Churches	SBC Share of Total CP	Total CP as % of Undes-ignated Gifts
1970s	9.94%	NA	8.97%	34.41%	N/A
1980s	7.58%	5.10%	6.83%	37.47%	10.50%
1990s	5.42%	4.91%	2.68%	37.04%	8.73%
2000s	4.12%	4.82%	2.23%	37.16%	6.80%
2010s	(0.21%)	0.71%	(1.16%)	39.34%	5.22%
Last 5 Yrs	0.65%	1.20%	(0.73%)	41.27%	4.79%

Chart prepared from the Southern Baptist Convention Annual of 2019 and Book of Reports, 2022.

SBC Missions (2010 - 2021)

Year	NAMB Cooperative Program	Annie Armstrong Offering	NAMB Missionaries
2010	$43,702,822	$52,415,505	5,096
2011	$43,729,142	$54,673,399	+2,616
2012	$43,683,642	$55,472,759	2,400
2013	$42,845,490	$54,957,016	2,406
2014	$42,518,758	$55,674,122	2,178
2015	$43,109,617	$55,610,226	++5,684
2016	$44,606,983	$56,056,232	5,684
2017	$45,894,865	$55,553,453	5,262
2018	$44,849,541	$56,668,218	5,097
2019	$44,835,155	$56,260,700	+++3,057
2020	$43,962,104	$43,502,420	2,218
2021	$43,773,080	$59,148,967	2,469

Year	IMB Cooperative Program	Lottie Moon Offering	IMB Missionaries
2010	$95,881,376	$145,662,925	5,031
2011	$95,939,322	$146,828,116	4,857
2012	$96,268,287	$149,276,303	4,850
2013	$94,376,650	$154,057,852	4,815
2014	$94,048,732	$153,002,394	4,792
2015	$95,362,518	$165,798,102	3.971
2016	$98,722,209	$152,982,560	3,596
2017	$98,792,233	*$14,766,873	3,563

2018	$99,347,638	$158,865,136	3,457
2019	$99,254,130	$157,300,000	3,615
2020	$97,241,319	$123,237,630	3,558
2021	$96,823,210	$128,285,813	3,592

*A change in IMB reporting dates provides only a partial year total in 2017.

+Beginning in 2011, NAMB non-appointed missionary spouses were no longer included in the count. Also, this year most of the reduction was due to eliminating most MSC (self-funded) missionaries

++Beginning in 2015, NAMB missionary count includes missionaries, church planters, church planting team members, and student missionaries.

+++Beginning in 2019, NAMB's missionary count fluctuates because most are church planters who rotate out five years after their church launches.

SBC Giving Trends (2010-2021)

Year	Total Receipts by SBC Churches	Total Undesignated Gifts to SBC Churches	Total CP
2010	$10,680,023,357	$8,911,796,522	$500,410,514
2011	$11,805,027,705	$9,023,216,896	$487,884,065
2012	$11,521,418,784	$8,891,673,582	$481,409,006
2013	$11,209,655,950	$8,769,026,657	$482,279,059
2014	$11,154,665,938	$8,748,114,744	$478,700,850
2015	$11,545,861,631	$9,154,427,472	$474,272,984
2016	$11,461,572,538	$9,216,198,700	$475,212,293
2017	$11,728,420,088	$9,518,527,051	$462,662,332
2018	$11,811,093,609	$9,601,534,950	$463,076,368
2019	$11,640,670,559	$9,600,108,179	$462,299,010
2020	$11,526,598,340	$9,531,225,749	$455,553,027
2021	$11,830,303,965	$9,774,807,128	$457,928,996

Year	Total State CP	Total SBC CP	Total CP % of Undesignated Gifts
2010	$308,647,361	$191,763,153	5.62%
2011	$301,498,029	$186,386,036	5.41%
2012	$294,768,525	$186,640,481	5.41%
2013	$298,859,256	$183,419,803	5.50%
2014	$297,729,271	$180,971,579	5.47%
2015	$290,501,682	$183,771,302	5.18%
2016	$284,743,512	$190,468,781	5.16%

2017	$270,713,506	$191,948,826	4.86%
2018	$271,818,380	$191,257,988	4.82%
2019	$271,331,607	$190,967,403	4.82%
2020	$267,746,391	$187,806,636	4.78%
2021	$270,153,074	$187,775,922	4.68%

Chart prepared from Annual of the Southern Baptist Convention, 2010-2021 and 2022 SBC Book of Reports (Executive Committee Reports).

Annual Great Commission Giving (2011-2021)

Year	Great Commission Giving
2011	$695,694,322
2012	$744,043,625
2013	$777,452,820
2014	$637,498,179
2015	$613,201,805
2016	$646,017,306
2017	$593,980,600
2018	$572,281,994
2019	$540,859,296
2020	$409,835,470
2021	$516,093,240

Chart prepared from Annual of the Southern Baptist Convention, 2010-2021 (EC Reports).

The SBC After GCR (2010-2021)

Year	Total Churches	Church Plants	Total Members	Total Baptisms
2010	45,727	769	16,136,044	331,008
2011	45,764	1,003	15,978,112	333,341
2012	46,034	927	15,872,404	314,956
2013	46,125	936	15,735,640	310,368
2014	46,499	985	15,499,173	305,301
2015	46,793	926	15,294,764	295,262
2016	47,272	732	15,216,978	280,773
2017	47,544	691	15,005,638	254,122
2018	47,456	624	14,813,234	246,442
2019	47,530	552	14,525,579	235,748
2020	47,592	588	14,089,947	123,160
2021	47,614	600	13,680,493	154,701

Year	Baptisms Per Church	Worship Attendance	SBC Share of CP	SBC CP
2010	7.2	6,195,449	38.32%	$191,763,153
2011	7.2	6,155,116	38.20%	$186,386,036
2012	6.8	5,966,735	38.77%	$186,640,481
2013	6.7	5,834.707	38.03%	$183,419,803
2014	6.5	5,674,469	37.80%	$180,971,579

2015	6.3	5,577,088	38.75%	$183,771,302
2016	5.9	5,200,716	40.08%	$190,468,781
2017	5.3	5,320,488	41.49%	$191,948,826
2018	5.1	5,297,788	41.30%	$191,257,988
2019	4.9	5,250,230	41.31%	$196,731,703
2020	2.5	4,439,797	41.23%	$187,806,636
2021	3.2	3,607,530	41.01%	$187,775,922

Table created by Dr. Chuck Kelley, New Orleans, Baptist Theological Seminary, from data in the Annuals of the SBC (2010-2022)

Non-CP Churches in the SBC (2010-2021)

Year	Total SBC Churches	Non-CP SBC Churches	% of Non-CP SBC Churches
2010	46,640	13,897	29.79%
2011	46,410	16,134	34.76%
2012	46,713	16,493	35.30%
2013	46,877	16,692	36.60%
2014	48,147	18,675	38.78%
2015	47,746	18,220	38.16%
2016	48,265	18,151	37.60%
2017	48,585	18,931	38.96%
2018	48,494	18,996	39.17%
2019	48,709	19,645	40.33%
2020			
2021			

Data from SBC Life Journal, Summer 2021 and Annuals of the Southern Baptist Convention

Church Planting Before GCR (2000-2010)

Year	Church Planting Budget	Church Planting Missionaries	New Church Plants
2000	$20,795,536	2,266	1,681*
2001	$21,260,083	2,262	1,415*
2002	$19,670,397	2,331	1,606*
2003	$19,489,287	2,273	1,436*
2004	$20,215,355	2,196	1,781*
2005	$17,478,713	2,023	1,725*
2006	$20,637,289	2,003	1,458*
2007	$23,937,093	2,228	1,455*
2008	$21,681,540	2,741	1,397*
2009	$21,409,697	2,734	1,256*
2010	$20,873,256	2,637	769

Source: Annuals of the Southern Baptist Convention
*Includes church plants and newly affiliated churches

Total Church Planting Budget 2000-2010: $227,448,246
Net Increase in SBC Churches 2000-2010: 4,139

Church Planting After GCR (2011-2021)

Year	Church Planting Budget	Church Planting Missionaries	New Church Plants
2011	$24,325,678	1,429	1,003
2012	$32,452,748	Not Released	927
2013	$62,296,234	Not Released	936
2014	$61,484,579	Not Released	985
2015	$72,455,657	Not Released	926
2016	$66,859,249	Not Released	732
2017	$69,681,886	Not Released	691
2018	$68,270,217	Not Released	624
2019	$66,985,421	Not Released	552
2020	$69,478,230	Not Released	588
2021	$73,101,916	1,316	600

Source: Annuals of the SBC & 2022 SBC Book of Reports

Total Church Planting Budget 2011-2020: $667,391,815
Net Increase in SBC Churches 2011-2020: 1,850

9 781953 331274